A Taste of BOSTON

The Definitive Cookbook of the City We Love

BILLY COSTA AND JENNY JOHNSON

Foreword by Mark Wahlberg

Photography by Brian Samuels

Jackson Point Publishing

Copyright ©2024 by Jenny Johnson and Billy Costa

All rights reserved. No part of this book may be used or reproduced in any manner whatsoever without written permission except in the case of brief quotations embodied in critical articles or reviews.

Published by Jackson Point Publishing

Hardcover ISBN: 979-8-9893952-3-1

Ebook ISBN: 979-8-9893952-4-8

Printed in the United States of America

10 9 8 7 6 5 4 3 2 1

Produced by GMK Writing and Editing, Inc.

Managing Editor: Katie Benoit

Contributor: Sara Farizan

Photographer: Brian Samuels, except where noted.

Food Tester: Catrine Kelly

Additional photos courtesy of Jenny Johnson, Spoonfuls, Camp Harbor View, The Food Project, The Greater Boston Food Bank, Michael Blanchard and Hancer Photography

Copyedited by Cindi Pietrzyk

Proofread by Kelly Nutter Clody

Text design and composition by Libby Kingsbury

Cover design by Libby Kingsbury

Jenny Johnson's hair by Danielle Davis

Jenny Johnson's makeup by Haylay Krull

Printed by IngramSpark

Thank you to everyone who has made the past twenty years possible, from the chefs to the waitstaffs to the restaurateurs, and to the many viewers who have come on this journey with us. And, of course, to our families, who have reminded us there is nothing better than being around a table with those you love.

ACKNOWLEDGMENTS

Much like a beautiful dish of food when it arrives at your table at a restaurant, a book is made possible by many hands that go entirely unseen by the reader. We are indebted to so many people who have not only made this book possible but who have also supported our career for decades. First and foremost, thank you to the extraordinary hospitality industry for welcoming us into your kitchens, dining rooms, and hotel lobbies for so many years. You have always given us the freshest ingredients to cook with, and we're grateful.

Going back to the very beginning of our wonderful partnership, we have to thank Charlie Kravetz for bringing us together and giving us the nudges we needed to find our dynamic.

Thank you to our countless partners. Your support enabled us to stay committed to storytelling and illuminate the many important, and often unsung, faces and places of our region. There are simply too many to list everyone, but we must acknowledge our longest standing premier partners: Joe Piantedosi, Joe Faro, Rob Waterman, Dan Donahue, Steve DiFillippo, Kristin Canty, Mike Rockett, Ernie Boch, Alan Gibeley, and Herb Chambers.

We've been blessed to have had the support and guidance of many friends and mentors over the years, including Dick Friedman, Tom Werner, John and Linda Henry, Sam Kennedy, Nicole Russo, JP Faiella, Bryan Barbieri, Lindsay Rotondi, Ryan Levasseur, Meghan O'Brien, Cameron Robbins, Dave Jacobs, Penelope Smith, Andrea Hutchins, Denise Cornish and Mark Bracken.

A heartfelt thank you to Martha Sheridan of Meet Boston for believing in a never-been-done-before idea and helping us bring it into reality. We're grateful to you and to your gifted team, especially Lindsay Milne, Cassandra Lee, Kate Davis, and Dave O'Donnell.

In so many ways, we are standing on the shoulders of our talented, creative, and diligent NESN team behind the scenes. Thank you Sean McGrail, Cosmina Schulman, Mike Crotty, Maddy Gaskill, Paul McLean, Calista Tufankjian, and Elyssa Hoffman. A special thanks to Kaila Tzianabos for your devotion over the years that enabled us to bring the brand to a new level. We can't wait to see all that you will do in the years to come.

Thank you to Gary Krebs, Kate Benoit, Libby Kingsbury, the calm and supremely talented Brian Samuels, and last but not least, Sara Farizan. Thank you for being so easy to trust and for helping us find our voices.

Billy's Acknowledgments:

The long list of people who have always been friends first, and partners second: Joe Piantedosi, Mike Rockett, Alan Gibeley, Steve DiFillippo, Joe Faro, Ernie Boch Jr., and Herb Chambers.

I have to give a shout out to my childhood friends who have supported me all these years: Dukey, Sandra Albano, John, Kate Campbell, my very first #l friend in life my brother Frank, and my absolute saint of a sister Patty.

Lisa Donovan, for standing by me and partnering in the morning with me, as well as the rest of the KISS 108 morning show team. Justin, Winnie, and producer Riley.

Thanks to the long list of iHeart executives, managers, producers, and interns who have stood by me and worked so hard for me.

Jenny Johnson, wow what to say? Your hard work, your sense of determination and drive are incredible. What a ride and adventure. Can we do twenty more years please?

My three sons, Chris, Alex, and Dylan, who will always be my biggest achievement.

My wife Michele, who is a never-ending source of love, support, and creative ideas when I need them.

Jenny's Acknowledgments:

Meredith Goldstein, for understanding me and my grandma. Benielle Sims, for introducing my girls to their favorite heroes. Jan Saragoni, for providing endless comic relief. Holly Finigan, for being the sand to my city. Tara Foley for our soul-fueling walks and talks among the trees. Samantha Devine, for seeing me and providing the safest space. Brehon, for your unbridled honesty—and for being there to flush. Erin, for the most loyal and loving commitment to friendship a girl could ever ask for.

It should go without saying, but a huge and heartfelt thank you to my partner-in-crime, Billy Costa. I can honestly say that I have not laughed more with anyone else in my life than you. Here's to many more.

Thank you to my extended Rotenberg tribe. In so many ways, growing up alongside you has made me the person I am today.

Thank you to the family I've gained—Louise, Stephen, and Mark Cocuzzo—for showering us with love and loyalty. To my brother-in-law Peter and nephew and niece Ollie and Henley, thank you for bringing so much laughter and joy into our lives. A deep heartfelt thank you to Arthur for your steadfast love and support.

And to my original nuclear, the impenetrable quartet. Zachary, for giving me maternal instincts long before I became a parent, for troubleshooting, for your loyalty and your unflappable and earnest positivity and charm. Hillary, can you play one more game before you go to sleep? My plus one for all of our twenties (and thirties) as we worked through it all. Thank you for your humor, your compassion, and your willingness. I am grateful for it all: the good, the hard, and the wild. Mom, Dali—my greatest teacher, the heart and soul, my North Star, my compass—you have my deepest gratitude for being the constant, the steady, the brave. I love you.

And last, but certainly not least, my heart. Lenox, you decisive warrior, I just hope the world is ready for you. Vienna, your passionate, theatrical imagery reminds me every day how present we can be. You smart, soulful, sweet girls—thank you for choosing me to be your mom. Rob, the half that has made me a whole in almost every single way. For all you've taught me and for all you've helped me feel, I love you.

And to you, the Reader:

We've been so grateful to have our seats at the table for so many years. Above all, we wanted this book to be a love letter, a long thank-you note to everyone who had welcomed us into their restaurants and into their homes. In sharing these stories and recipes, we are trying to give back for all that we have been given. With that said...can we see a dessert menu?

Contents

Foreword xv
Introduction 1

Breakfast 5

Lydia Shire 6
    Kedegree

Jose Duarte 9
    Pan con Chicharrón

Garrett Harker 13
    Eastern Standard's Butterscotch Bread Pudding

Erin Miller 17
    Laminated Buttermilk Biscuits with Apple Butter

Lambert Givens and Nick Dixon 22
    Liège Waffles with Peach Cobbler Topping

Douglass Williams 26
    Shakshuka

Matt King 31
    Lobster Latkes with Horseradish Sour Cream, Poached Eggs, and Caviar

Michael Schlow 36
    Maine Crab Tartare with Cucumber and Cilantro

Anthony Caturano 39
    Cottage Cheese Pancakes

Jen and Josh Ziskin 43
    Salt Cod Potato Cakes

Michael Lombardi 48
    Bacon Potato Gruyère Pizza

Jeremy Sewall 53
    Poached Eggs with Prosciutto, Arugula, Tomatoes, and Salsa Verde

Deborah Hansen 56
    Lemon Olive Oil Cake

Tom Berry 59
    Mulberry French Toast

Mark Cina and Tom Schlesinger-Guidelli 63
    Smoked Ham Grits Benedict

Marc Orfaly 67
    Tipico Montanero

Lunch 73

Tiffani Faison 74
Buttermilk Fried Chicken Sandwich with Smoked Jalapeño Goo

Ken Oringer 80
Coppa's Nduja Pizza

Carl Dooley 84
Lamb Burger with Pickled Cauliflower and Tomato Chutney

Jatinder Singh and Supreet Kaur 89
Shahi Navratan Korma

Andy Husbands 92
Pork Belly Banh Mi

Paul Wahlberg 96
Seared Salmon with Rhubarb Vinaigrette, Black Rice, and Minted Cucumber

Joe Milano and Americo DiFronzo 98
New England Lobster Roll with French Fries

Joe Faro and Nimesh Maharjan 103
Cacio e Pepe

Brendan Pelley 107
Sourdough Bread Bar Vlaha Style

Colton Coburn-Wood 111
Conchita Pibil Tacos

Jason Santos 115
Chicken and Waffle Tacos with Lime Syrup, Watermelon Pico de Gallo, and Avocado Butter

Chris Himmel and Robert Sisca 120
Ribeye, Butter-Poached Lobster, Caramelized Onions, and Watercress

Nancy and Tim Cushman 124
Hojoko Wasabi Roulette Sushi

Asia Mei 129
Good Luck Lumpia with Shrimp and Ground Turkey Filling

Patricia Estorino 133
Empandas de Picadillo (Ground Beef Empanadas)

Thanaphon "Song" Authaiphan 137
Green Papaya Pad Thai

Pam and Chris Willis 140
Spaghetti Squash and Buratta

Frank DePasquale and Nello Caccioppoli 144
Wild Boar

Dinner 149

Ana Sortun 150
    Topik

Kristin Canty and Charlie Foster 154
    Crispy Lamb Ribs

Karen Akunowicz 160
    Orecchiette con Cime di Rapa

Cassie Piuma 165
    Steak Gyros with Black Truffle Tzatziki

Steve DiFillippo and Rodney Murillo 169
    Kobe Meatballs

Tatiana Rosana 174
    Paella de Mariscos

Nia Grace 177
    Hot Maryland Crab Dip

Jesus Preciado 180
    Uvetsi

Michael Serpa 183
    Whole Roasted Sea Bream "Taverna Style"

The Nebo Sisters 186
    Polenta con Scampi Fritti

Kwasi Kwaa 190
    Jollof Rice with Ginger Red Wine Braised Goat

Jody Adams 194
    Ricotta Gnocchi with Mushrooms

David Daniels 199
    Nantucket Bay Scallops in the Style of Our Meunière

Haley Fortier and Kathryn Britten 202
    Duck Rillette

Tony Susi 205
    Squash Tortelli, Brown Butter, Toasted Almonds, Pecorino Romano Fonduta

Brian Moy 208
    Bò Lúc Lác (Vietnamese Shaking Beef)

Andrew Hebert 213
    Charred Cabbage "Mozambique" with Garlic, Chili, and Cerveja

Dessert 217

Joanne Chang 218
    Boston Cream Pie

Kathy Sidell and Ben Sidell 224
    Pistachio Tiramisu

Maura Kilpatrick 229
    Sesame Cashew Bar

Sarah Wade 233
    Ricotta Donuts with Honey Rum Sauce

Rachel Sundet 236
    Honey Cake

Renae Connolly and Michael Pagliarini 239
    Gooey Chocolate Cakes with Ricotta Frosting

Holly Safford 244
    Espresso Martini Coconut Macaroons

Abdulla Awad 248
    Almondo

Will Gilson and Brian Mercury 251
    Pistachio Citrus Cheesecake

Julie Freitas 255
    Sugar Baking Co. Hermits

Bios 259

FOREWORD

by Mark Wahlberg

Food was always a focal point of my childhood growing up in Dorchester.
I, along with my eight brothers and sisters would pile around the table, and my mom would come out of the kitchen with one of her signature dishes. Feeding all those mouths, she knew how to do a lot with a little—and did it well.

We all had our favorites. Donnie loved her fried chicken wings. Paul's favorite was her English muffin pizza (funny to think he became the chef of the bunch!). Tracy's was her shepherd's pie. My favorite was always her lasagna with ricotta cheese and homemade tomato sauce. Up until the last years of her life, I'd ask my mom to make that lasagna whenever I went home to Boston. Just the thought of those flavors keeps me connected to her today.

Food is the gateway to our most cherished memories. And in Boston, there's no shortage of memory-making at the many world-class restaurants we have. Of course, I have my go-to spots—pasta at Davio's, lobsters at Legal. Obviously, I know where to go for the best burger in town. But sometimes even I need a recommendation, and I've always known who to turn to for that.

Billy Costa and I go *waaay* back to my early days. He's been the voice of Boston's music scene at Kiss 108 for decades. But after he teamed up with his co-host Jenny Johnson and created what is today NESN's *Dining Playbook*, Billy and Jenny have served as the voice of Boston's restaurant scene. They have been promoting Boston's restaurants for more than two decades. They are generous to local businesses and essential cheerleaders for chefs and restaurateurs, who have some of the toughest jobs in the world.

When my family and I started Wahlburgers, Billy and Jenny were at our openings and promoted our restaurants as we expanded. They have been huge supporters in highlighting our restaurant Alma Nove in Hingham. They even cooked with my mom!

As they've done for so many chefs, they helped tell my brother Paul's story for years. If any of my other family members needed to promote a cause or needed hosts for a gala or charity event, they were there. When I needed someone to play a local journalist in one of my movies, Jenny hit her mark, took direction, and knew how to work the camera. When I came to Boston to promote my tequila—Flecha

Azul—Billy and Jenny had a hand in making sure the place was packed. After Billy introduced me to the crowd, we toasted the old days.

Our family aside, Billy and Jenny give just as much attention to local folks. They know the bartenders, the waiters, and managers of joints from the Back Bay to the Seaport. But they especially love the chefs. What makes them different is that they don't just tell the story of the food; they tell the story of the person behind the recipe. That is why this cookbook is so special.

A Taste of Boston doesn't just give you recipes to make memories with, it introduces you to the characters who dreamed them up. In this way, these dishes transcend simply being something to cook and eat. They are experiences meant to be savored. I'll bet you'll find a dish in here that you'll never forget, just like Mom's lasagna.

INTRODUCTION

What makes a partnership last the test of time? We'd say it's a rare recipe: one part humor, one part patience, a heaping dose of trust, and a sprinkling of magic. When fate brought us together twenty years ago—Billy, a legendary Boston DJ and Emmy-nominated TV host, and Jenny, then a recent college grad hungry to break into the media industry as an associate producer—we had no idea that those special ingredients were coming together.

We both vividly remember sitting in the office of Charlie Kravitz, then president of New England Cable News (NECN). Charlie was looking for an associate producer for Billy's weekly show *TV Diner*, a half-hour program that took viewers into the best restaurants around the city. In the course of that hour-long meeting, sparks flew like flames from a chef's scorching-hot sauté pan. The chemistry was obvious. Billy turned to Charlie and said, "Well, the search is over."

Twenty years later, it is humbling (and baffling!) to think we are the longest-running male/female broadcasting duo in the history of Boston. Part of what has kept us together is our shared vision. We were always on the same page about how much we admire the people featured on our shows. We never wanted to critique or rate their restaurants. Instead, we committed to celebrating these hard-working, creative, and gifted individuals.

The culinary scene in Boston would not be where it is today without the influence of those who paved the way—chefs such as Gordon Hamersley, Chris Schlesinger, Jacky Robert, Lydia Shire, Ming Tsai, and the late Jasper White to name a few. We have been fortunate to call many of these chefs dear friends today. They set the tradition that today's up-and-coming culinary masters are carrying forward to bold, new frontiers.

Over the years, we noticed something striking. Food was one of the most important ways people came together in Boston. The chefs and restaurateurs were the curators of community. As hosts of a local TV show, we had a bigger job than we originally thought. The restaurants we were spotlighting—well before there were influencers or social media tastemakers—were a huge part of our local economy and culture. We realized we were part of promoting the culinary ecosystem, and we took our responsibility to support those feeding the city very seriously—with some laughs along the way, of course.

We recognized we had front-row seats to the burgeoning careers of chefs who would become major stars. We interviewed them before shows such as *Top Chef* and *Chopped* even existed. We were there when they opened their first restaurants. We were there to celebrate when they mentored others who did the same. When the world began to notice Boston as a prominent culinary scene, we already knew and had championed all the people who had made that happen.

We've been fiercely loyal to not only the chefs and restaurateurs, but also to each other. Our professional journey has been a personal one. We've become more than co-hosts over the last twenty years—we're family. We've experienced every stage of life together. Billy was Jenny's Man of Honor at her wedding and is an honorary uncle to her daughters Vienna and Lenox. When it was time to celebrate Billy's big birthdays over the years, Jenny was a part of planning. And when Billy's sons were young, Jenny was a member of their support village helping shuttle the boys to hockey. We've been through both triumphs and tribulations, but have always remained committed to one another.

When *TV Diner* ended ten years ago, we knew we wanted to continue telling the stories of the people who made up the heartbeat of our city. With the blessing and support of Red Sox Chairman Tom Werner, who also runs New England Sports Network (NESN), we launched our next show: *Dining Playbook*. With that, we had new reach and an ever-expanding audience as we helped usher in a new wave of culinary greatness.

After twenty years, we're proud to still be part of the hospitality scene in Boston. With viewers, as well as restaurateurs and businesses, wanting our insight on a regular basis, we wanted to record this moment in time. To commemorate twenty years of recipes, TV segments, and friendships, we decided it was time to give you our *A Taste of Boston*. To us, the work we've done together is a gift. We made this book as a gift for *you*.

We wanted to honor the unique talent that has made Boston what it is and helps it continue to grow. We wanted to give you a guide to places you should experience while you're here. We wanted to honor *you*, all the chefs at home, who want to try some of the best recipes you'll ever eat. We saw a unique opportunity to get sixty of the most talented and award-winning minds in hospitality to offer us a recipe. Their enthusiastic participation makes us so proud. The chefs recognized that in us sharing their stories over the years, we also became a part of *their* stories.

This treasure trove of recipes for breakfast, lunch, dinner, and dessert are rare, highly coveted, and appreciated. We hope you'll come along as we take you on a culinary tour of our favorite place on Earth. It's been an honor to be cheerleaders for everyone who enjoys the world of food in this great city. You are what make it so special . . . and delicious.

Lastly, we are still going strong in huge part because of our partners. Thank you to NESN for your eleven years of support and to Meet Boston for helping us to elevate our programming to the next level. This book was made possible by both of these tremendous organizations.

Enjoy and dig in!

—Billy and Jenny

Breakfast

LYDIA SHIRE

In this job, we've been lucky enough to spend time with many talented chefs with prestigious resumes. Lydia Shire is a step above. When she's around, we feel *in our bones* that we are in the presence of culinary royalty. We've wanted to soak up every second we've been with her, especially when she's holding court in her kitchen.

The James Beard Award–winning chef was born and raised in Brookline, to two illustrator parents, which proves that artistry runs in the family. She's shattered pretty much every glass ceiling a woman can in the fine-dining scene. She started as a "salad girl" (yes, that's what they called them) at Boston's Maison Robert, studied at London's Cordon Bleu, returned to Maison Robert, and eventually became the restaurant's head chef. She went on to be the Bostonian Hotel's first female chef, where she was mentored and befriended by the late, great legend Jasper White.

She was the first female executive chef to open a Four Seasons luxury property during her time at the Four Seasons Hotel Beverly Hills in the 1980s. Thankfully, she came back to Boston and helped put the city on the culinary map by winning national awards, helming a pack of restaurants with inventive menus, and mentoring chefs who would become crucial to the city, such as Gordon Hamersley, Jody Adams, Susan Regis, Dante de Magistris, and Amanda Lydon. She credits the late, great Moncef Meddeb as her Boston culinary mentor, and did we mention she was also dear friends with *the* Julia Child? Like we said, *culinary royalty*.

As regal as Chef Shire is, she's never one to shy away from sharing a laugh, and she's always been generous with her time and talent, especially when it comes to charitable events. When we hosted one of our first galas together, we approached Chef Shire knowing that if she was on the lineup, the gala would be a go. Not only did her participation guarantee the event would happen, it encouraged *many* others to take part in the event.

As executive chef and co-owner of Scampo in the Liberty Hotel, Chef Shire continues to wow with a seasonally changing menu of Italian-inspired delicacies and dishes that feature Middle Eastern and Mediterranean influences. Her youngest son, Alex Pineda, who worked alongside her at Scampo, carries on his mother's royal lineage as he reigns over his own kitchens.

Chef Shire is also a collector. Not just of things, but of memories. Jenny was fortunate to visit Lydia's home for an interview and came across the most intricate, ornate, and rare culinary items. From vintage spoons to antique wine glasses, every object had a story. Chef Shire is the same way with recipes; each meal in her Rolodex is connected to stories and people that have changed her life—and the city.

We hope we're on a card in her Rolodex of memories, too. It would be an honor.

KEDEGREE

Serves 4

This dish features a wonderful aromatic rice originally from South India with smoked fish, curry, and sublime six-minute eggs. Kedegree landed in Britain and is much beloved by all.

1. Bring medium saucepan of water to boil. Gently lower eggs into water. Lower the heat to a gentle simmer and cook for 6 minutes only (the yolks will be slight runny). Remove pan from heat, drain water and peel the eggs. Set aside.

2. In a large saucepan, add rice, water, and pinch of salt. Bring to a boil over high heat. Reduce heat to a simmer and continue to cook, covered, for about 5 minutes. Remove pan from the heat. Let sit, covered, for about 10 minutes.

3. Have about 3 cups of boiling water ready. Place fish in another large saucepan. Add cream and celery leaves. Pour in just enough boiling water to cover the fish and bring to a simmer over medium heat. Reduce heat to medium-low and continue to cook, uncovered, until the thickest part of the fish turns opaque, about 6 minutes. Do not overcook.

4. Remove fish from the cream. Discard the cream. When the fish is cool enough to handle, break into large chunks, keeping the celery leaves but discarding any bones. Keep the skin if you prefer (I do). Set fish aside.

5. Melt 2 ounces butter in a large Dutch oven or heavy-duty casserole dish. Add onions, cover, and cook over medium-low heat, stirring occasionally, until the onions soften, about 10 minutes. Add curry powder, cardamom pods, and bay leaves. Continue to cook, stirring occasionally until the mixture is well combined, about 2 minutes.

6. Add the prepared rice, stirring to combine. This is the point to taste the rice. Add salt, pepper or butter as necessary.

7. Gently fold in the fish.

8. Quarter the eggs (remember, the yolks should be slightly runny), and lay them on top of your rice on a platter of your choice.

9. Sprinkle generously with the parsley and cilantro.

10. Add lemon juice and season with salt and pepper. Garnish with lemon wedges, if desired.

---

4 large eggs

6 ounces (about 7/8 cup) basmati rice, rinsed

1 cup cold water

Kosher salt, to taste

1 pound smoked haddock or smoked sable fish (Whole Foods is a good source for this.)

8 ounces heavy cream

1/2 cup inner pale celery leaves

2 ounces (4 tablespoons) unsalted butter, more to taste

2 large onions, finely sliced, about 2½ to 3 cups

4 teaspoons good, strong Madras curry powder

6 cardamom pods crushed

2 bay leaves

Freshly ground black pepper, to taste

1/4 cup finely chopped curly parsley, for garnish

1/4 cup rough chopped cilantro, for garnish

1½ tablespoons freshly squeezed lemon juice

Lemon wedges, optional

JOSE DUARTE

The best teachers are the ones who make learning fun. That's why we love Jose Duarte, our favorite educator. He's a chef-owner whose brain works at lightning speed. He has long been invested in sustainability and has introduced us to concepts and foods before they became wildly popular.

Today, everyone can pronounce *quinoa* (or most of us can), but on a shoot almost twenty years ago, Jose was using the ingredient when it was still new to the rest of us. It took Billy a while to learn to say the Q-word, but with Jose's patience and infectious enthusiasm, Billy eventually got there.

Jose was the one who taught us about pisco sour and what we should consider "real deal" ceviche. He also taught us that fusion could be on a whole other level when he and his lovely wife Anna (who owns Trattoria San Pietro in Norwell) opened Taranta in the North End in 2000. Jose was blending classic Italian fare with flavors from Peru, whipping up an amalgamation of ingredients that were as colorful, wonderful, and inventive as its chef.

We've traveled with him locally and internationally for the show and on our own, and it's always a master class. Whether it's riding around the streets of Boston as Jose is feeding us dishes from the backseat, in the marketplaces of Rome, or amid the gorgeous landscape of Machu Pichu, he can talk about any neighborhood and its significance to cuisine. We also know that wherever he takes us will *not* be on our travel itinerary.

When we were together in Rome for a shoot years ago, Jose took us to off-the-beaten-path grocery stores—places we'd never find on our own. He'd get to know the people who worked at the fruit stand while showing us a piece of produce, tearing it apart, describing its benefits, and explaining the history and alchemy of how it was grown. Jose knows many languages and even taught us to swear in Italian! (This is a family-friendly book, so we will not share what we learned, but it comes in handy.)

Maybe it's because he's such a global citizen—and because he and his family travel all over the world—that he's always been on the forefront of green solutions to make the hospitality industry more eco-friendly. We remember many years ago when Jose pulled up to meet us in a large pickup truck that was powered by used kitchen grease! Since then, his commitment to sustainability has been recognized with numerous awards, including the 2008 City of Boston Green Business Award and the 2011 Massachusetts Recycling Award, to name a few.

He has also never forgotten his roots and created the Santa Cruz Eco Lodge in Peru, a beautiful twelve-bedroom hotel and restaurant in the foothills of the Huascaran National Park. The lodge is designed for guests to enjoy the nature of the Andean Mountains and for the agricultural community of Huaripampa to thrive by growing food naturally. He teaches us all about how tourism can best serve guests and the climate by using renewable energy and local produce, and by being beneficial to the local population.

If you can't make it to Peru, might we suggest visiting Tambo 22, Jose and Anna's restaurant in Chelsea. You'll get authentic Peruvian dishes, and if you're lucky enough, Chef Jose may be there to teach you how the dish you're enjoying made it to your plate.

PAN CON CHICHARRÓN

Serves 4

Pan con chicharrón is a specially prepared Peruvian pork sandwich where the main ingredient is fried in its own fat. Chicharrón, regardless of its main ingredient, is a true delight. In Peru, it takes center stage during breakfast.

To roast the belly

1. Place the pork belly, skin side up in a deep dish. Score the skin 1 inch apart with the tip of a razor blade or utility knife. This helps remove excess water for a crispy texture.

2. Season the top of the belly with coarse sea salt; cover with plastic wrap and refrigerate overnight.

3. The next day, preheat the oven to 250°F.

4. Remove any excess liquid by drying the skin with a paper towel. Place the belly in a deep roasting pan, place in the oven, and slow roast for 2¼ hours. Then increase the temperature to 450°F for about 5 minutes until the skin becomes crispy, achieving the crackling "chicharrón" effect. If the skin does not get crispy, put under the oven broil to crisp; watch carefully so that it doesn't burn.

Remove from oven and let it cool for a few minutes.

To make the fried sweet potatoes

1. Heat vegetable oil in large frying pan and add sweet potato slices, turning until golden brown and tender. Sprinkle with salt as desired.

2. Remove with a slotted spoon onto a plate lined with paper towels to drain oil.

To make the salsa criolla topping

1. In a large bowl, lightly mix onion, mint, lime juice, and vinegar.

To assemble the sandwiches

1. Place the cooked pork belly on a cutting board, crispy skin side up. Using a serrated bread knife, cut into 1-inch slices.

2. Lightly toast the banh mi roll. Cut the rolls in half and place the fried sweet potatoes on the bottom, then the pork belly, and then the criolla salad. Place the top of the roll on and press lightly to keep the ingredients in the roll. Repeat with the remaining three rolls.

---

1 pound fresh pork belly, skin on

Coarse sea salt, to taste

1 large sweet potato, peeled and cut into 1-inch-thick lengthwise pieces

1/2 cup vegetable oil

Salt, to taste

1 large red onion, thinly sliced

1/2 cup chopped mint leaves

Juice of 2 limes

1 tablespoon white vinegar

4 banh mi rolls (Vietnamese baguette) or a regular baguette cut in 4

GARRETT HARKER

It is safe to say there would be no Kenmore Square restaurant scene without Garrett Harker.

Sure, the lively intersection near Boston University and Fenway Park existed before Garrett, but it became a foodie's dream when restaurateur Harker opened Eastern Standard and changed the entire taste of the neighborhood.

After opening in 2005, Eastern Standard became the place for every occasion. If you had tickets to a Sox game, a business meeting that required comfort but class, or needed a quiet spot for after-dinner drinks with a friend you hadn't seen in years, Eastern Standard was it.

When he launched, he launched *big*, and immediately commanded the respect of the city and the culinary world of greater Boston.

It's no surprise that Eastern Standard became an anchor of the culinary scene so quickly. Garrett had been the man behind No. 9 Park, B&G Oysters, and The Butcher Shop. He also helped shape a generation of restaurateurs, including Tom Schlesinger-Guidelli and Andrew Holden, among others.

We can always tell who's been mentored by Garrett because of the way they welcome and attend to guests like Garrett does. When Garrett greets you at one of his restaurants, he's the ultimate positive-energy extrovert.

A Taste of Boston

He cups his hands together while gently leaning forward to listen attentively to a guest, and we've seen his mentees do the same. He's a steward of hospitality to everyone he encounters.

We have no idea how Garrett keeps it all straight in his head. It's like he knows every guest like family, remembering when they were last in and who they brought. He's that way with neighborhood regulars, college students on a budget, and big names in the city.

Always reinventing and evolving, Garrett has had many chapters in his decades-long, James Beard–nominated career. We're a huge fan of his side business, Eastern Standard Provisions, which makes the softest, tastiest pretzels (you can find them at his places and restaurants around the city). If you don't want to take our word for it, Garrett's pretzels are Oprah-approved, making one of her Favorite Things lists.

Eastern Standard closed in its original location in 2020. We're grateful it came back down the street in 2023. His regulars were thrilled to see their favorite timeless menu and feel the Eastern Standard charm.

Stop in if you want to see a gracious friend who helped shape the city. Garrett will be happy to welcome you back.

EASTERN STANDARD'S BUTTERSCOTCH BREAD PUDDING

Serves 10 to 12

This amazing bread pudding features a beautiful custard on the bottom with crispy bread on top. It is delicious served warm with praline ice cream or whipped cream!

- 1 tablespoon butter, for greasing
- 1 loaf brioche, cut in 1/2-inch cubes
- 2 quarts half-and-half
- 2 cups granulated sugar
- 6 yolks
- 6 eggs
- 24 ounces butterscotch chips

1. Grease a 9- x 13-inch dish with butter, set aside.

2. Spread brioche cubes in a single layer on a baking sheet and bake for 15 minutes, turning pan around halfway during baking, until cubes are nicely toasted.

3. Transfer toasted cubes to prepared baking dish, set aside.

4. In small saucepan over medium heat, bring half-and-half and sugar to a simmer, making sure not to boil.

5. In the meantime, combine eggs and yolks together in a large bowl and put butterscotch chips in another large bowl.

6. Slowly add half of the half-and-half mixture to the egg mixture one cup at a time, stirring constantly. This process tempers the eggs to avoid cooking them. Add the remaining half-and-half to the egg mixture.

7. Put a fine mesh strainer over the bowl of butterscotch chips and pour the egg and half-and-half mixture over.

8. Whisk until the chips have melted and the mixture is smooth.

9. Pour the mixture over the bread, pushing the bread into the liquid with a fork.

10. Cover with plastic wrap and let soak overnight in the refrigerator.

11. When ready to bake, preheat the oven to 325°F.

12. Remove plastic wrap and cover bread pan with sprayed aluminum foil.

13. Put the pan on a rimmed baking sheet and make a water bath by adding water halfway up the pan. Bake for 1 hour.

14. Remove foil and bake an additional half hour until the top is golden and the edges are crispy. Chill and then cut. Can be chilled in fridge for 4 hours up to overnight.

ERIN MILLER

What do you usually tell your friends about a night of dining out? You talk about the main dishes, who you were with, the ambience, and the service. After a night at Urban Hearth, you'll also talk about the bread.

Elsewhere, it might be an afterthought—a warm up to a great meal—but at Urban Hearth, it's a main attraction. If you've had it, you know what we're talking about. Yes, technically, it's a biscuit. It's also perfection.

We'll get back to the carbs in a second, because we should tell you about Chef Erin Miller and her restaurant first. The idea for Urban Hearth began while Chef Miller was operating her own private event company. Executive chef and owner Miller combined her skills from her time at the French Culinary Institute in New York with her experience working in restaurants to create amazing farm-to-table dining experiences, which she then brought into people's homes.

The brick-and-mortar version of her vision, Urban Hearth, opened in 2016 and is designed to make guests feel like they've gone out, but are having a cozy night *in*. They can find comfort in contemporary American foods that look and feel familiar, but always have a global twist. Chef Miller's menu is globally inspired and seasonally driven.

It's an ever-changing à la carte menu that pairs foods we've never seen together on the same fork. Recent plates include Celery Root Crème Brûlée, Crispy Confit Duck Leg in a Sunchoke Mole with Broccolini and Pomegranate, and Scallops in Green Apple Leche de Tigre.

The ingredients are intentionally locally sourced, which makes us feel like we're supporting the entire industry as diners. If you order the tasting menu, or reserve the restaurant for a private event, you'll get a chance to sit at the chef's counter and see Erin running the kitchen. Those lucky people get to chat with Chef Miller as she cooks. Her cuisine, and how she thinks about what to create and where it comes from, make being at Urban Hearth an educational experience. She's as thoughtful with her plating as she is as a person.

Chef Miller, with her husband and two sons, call Cambridge home, and we wonder if her family is as amazed by her biscuits as we are—especially with a side of apple butter!

LAMINATED BUTTERMILK BISCUITS WITH APPLE BUTTER

Makes approximately 12 medium-size biscuits

These biscuits are flaky, buttery, and perfect for breakfast in bed or having friends over for brunch.

To make the biscuits

1. Grate cold butter with the large-hole side of a box grater onto parchment paper. Transfer paper and butter to an airtight container and put in the freezer for a minimum of 30 minutes.

2. In a large mixing bowl, whisk together flour, baking powder, salt and sugar.

3. Add frozen butter.

4. Using your hands and a gentle touch, toss the butter with the flour until butter is broken up and distributed throughout the flour mixture.

5. Using a rubber pastry scraper or spatula, begin pouring buttermilk into the butter/flour mixture approximately 1/4 cup at a time, mixing gently after each pour and rotating the bowl so the next pour falls onto dry ingredients (similar to making pastry crust).

6. When all the buttermilk is added, continue to gently toss the ingredients until the mixture is mostly clumped together. Mixture will still be loose and dry looking.

7. Dump the mixture onto the work surface and, using your hands or a metal bench scraper, gently form the mass into a flat rectangle about 2 inches thick and oriented vertically in front of you.

8. Pull out a piece of cling film long enough to cover twice the length of your rectangle and lay it over the top of the dough.

9. Using a rolling pin, gently roll the dough from the center up and then from the center down, roll in the same fashion side to side, maintaining the general shape of the rectangle to about 1-inch thickness. Remove cling film.

10. Using a large spatula or your metal bench scraper, fold the rectangle in thirds, like a letter. Fold the top of the rectangle to the center and then fold the bottom up and over the top section. The dough will fragment—that's okay! Just piece it back together and pat gently.

11. Rotate the dough clockwise by 90 degrees so your horizontal rectangle is now vertical again.

For the biscuits

- 1⅓ cups unsalted butter, cold
- 5⅓ cups all-purpose flour
- 2½ tablespoons baking powder
- 1½ teaspoons kosher salt
- 1½ tablespoons granulated sugar
- 2 cups (16 fluid ounces) buttermilk

For the apple butter

- 2 pounds mixed apples (approximately 4 apples, e.g., Gala, Macintosh, Cortland), peeled, cored, and diced.
- 3/4 cup apple cider (or water)
- 1 tablespoon freshly squeezed lemon juice or cider vinegar
- 1/4 cup granulated sugar, or less depending on taste
- 1/4 cup brown sugar, or less depending on taste
- 1/2 teaspoon ground cinnamon
- 1/8 teaspoon ground clove
- 1/4 teaspoon kosher salt

12. Cover with plastic wrap and repeat the same rolling, folding, and turning technique two more times for a total of three "turns."

13. Slide dough onto a baking sheet, cover loosely with plastic wrap, and place in the refrigerator for 20 to 30 minutes to rest.

14. Preheat the oven to 400°F (375°F with convection). Move the rack to the lowest position.

15. After the dough has rested, remove from the refrigerator. Dust your work surface with a light coating of flour. Turn the dough over onto the floured work surface.

16. Complete three more "turns," using your bench scraper to even the edges and keep the shape of the rectangle as you work.

17. After completing the sixth turn, cover and return your dough to the refrigerator for another 30 minutes of rest.

18. Return dough to your dusted work surface, and rolling from the center out, roll the dough gently to about 1-inch thickness.

19. Using a long sharp knife or a pizza cutter, cut the dough lengthwise into three long strips. Then cut the strips in the opposite direction into 4 equal pieces. You should end up with about 12 medium-size squares.

20. Line your baking sheet with parchment paper, transfer the cut biscuits to the baking sheet, allowing a couple inches of space between each biscuit.

Place immediately into the oven on the lowest rack and bake for about 15 minutes until biscuits are golden brown and cooked through. These are delicious served warm with Apple Butter!

To make the apple butter

1. Combine chopped apples, apple cider, and lemon juice in a medium saucepot with a tight-fitting lid.

2. Bring apple mixture to a simmer, and continue to cook at a vigorous pace until apples are very soft and falling apart, 25 to 30 minutes.

3. Add sugar, spices, and salt to apple sauce, stir to combine.

4. Continue to cook, uncovered, at a steady simmer until sauce is reduced and glossy, stirring occasionally, 45 to 60 minutes.

5. Store in an airtight container in the refrigerator. Apple butter will keep for up to 3 weeks.

CHEF'S TIP: If you would like to freeze all or part of your biscuit batch, place uncooked biscuits in a container lined with parchment (separate with 2 sheets of parchment if stacking is required). Make sure the container is tightly sealed and place in the freezer for up to a month. Allow biscuits to thaw at room temperature for about 20 minutes before baking.

CHEF'S TIP: Make sure your prep table is clean and you have plenty of room, and it's always a good idea to read all the directions before proceeding with a recipe!

LAMBERT GIVENS AND NICHOLAS DIXON

Sometimes people ask us where young people go in Boston. We aren't in that demographic anymore, but we can say quite confidently, it's Southie.

If you're over fifty, that might surprise you. But if you're in your twenties and thirties, you know South Boston is a *haven* for young professionals who expect great food and cocktails to be part of their nightlife scene.

How did Southie become the hotspot for young millennials and beyond?

We give major credit to Broadway Restaurant Group—specifically our friends Eric Aulenback, who owns all of the group's restaurants, Chef Nick Dixon, and Chef Lambert Givens.

Picture it: It's a Friday night in South Boston. The streets are busy. You'll see friends snacking on tacos at Loco Taqueria & Oyster Bar, two people on a date eating sushi at Fat Baby, a pack of sports fans lining up outside Lincoln Tavern and Restaurant to watch the Pats while noshing on pizza and burgers, and scenesters waiting in line for pasta at Capo before heading to the supper club downstairs to listen to live music, take selfies, and dance. In the morning they all might go to a Southern-inspired brunch at Hunter's.

All of these are Broadway Restaurant Group businesses, and they all serve tasty cuisine.

The Broadway Restaurant Group is led by restaurateur Eric Aulenback, who, along with his partners, have done a neighborhood reinvention more than once. After Southie, it was Charlestown with spots like Monument Restaurant & Tavern, Prima Boston Italian Steakhouse, and Waverly Kitchen and Bar (which serves brunch seven days a week and has the best banana bread that should never be taken off the menu!).

A big secret to the success is Chef Dixon, who started his career with the group at Lincoln Tavern. As a kid in Hanover, Massachusetts, Dixon helped his executive chef father with kitchen prep at Red Coach Bar & Grill. After graduating from Brookline's Newbury College School of Culinary Studies, he got a job with The Lyons Group, a dining and entertainment behemoth in Boston. This is where Eric and Nicholas met, working together in ten restaurants over a fifteen-year period. Though Chef Dixon worked at other restaurants in the area as well as Las Vegas in between their partnership, when he returned home, they hit the ground running.

Chef Dixon is now the culinary director of the Broadway Restaurant Group, and the team includes another heavy hitter, Chef Lambert Givens, affectionately nicknamed Chef Lambo. A former South Carolina State University football player and business grad, Chef Givens mentored with Dixon and became the executive chef at Hunter's Kitchen & Bar. There he serves comfort food inspired by his childhood in Connecticut where he learned family recipes from his grandmother and parents, who had roots in Georgia and Alabama. Be sure to order Lambo's Gumbo, which *Beat Bobby Flay*.

Now, we know we said Southie is a neighborhood for the young and hip, but don't let that scare you away. We dine there before eight at night, and we feel right at home.

LIÈGE WAFFLES WITH PEACH COBBLER TOPPING

Serves 5

Peach cobbler is a Southern classic that is amazing when served at Hunter's Kitchen & Bar. It's even better when served on a waffle.

To make the waffles

1. In a bowl combine milk, warm water, brown sugar, and yeast. Using a whisk, mix all ingredients together until combined. Set mixture aside for 5 minutes to allow yeast to dissolve.

2. Once the yeast is dissolved, pour milk mixture into the mixing bowl of a small stand mixer, add eggs, extract, salt, and flour. Using a dough hook, mix ingredients together on speed 1 until dough begins to form a ball around the dough hook.

3. With the mixer on speed 1, slowly add a piece of butter into the dough. Once that piece is incorporated into the dough, add the next. Continue until all butter has been added and fully incorporated.

4. Remove dough from the mixer; place into an oil-sprayed bowl. Cover the bowl with plastic wrap and leave at room temp for 1 hour.

5. Remove dough from the bowl and place onto a lightly flour surface. Sprinkle pearl sugar over the top and knead it into the dough until it is fully combined.

6. Divide the dough into approximately 5 1-cup balls.

7. Place 1 dough ball into the center of a preheated waffle iron and cook until waffle is golden brown. Repeat with other 4 dough balls.

To make the topping

1. In a saucepan, combine the peaches, sugar, cinnamon, nutmeg, butter, and water.

2. Place the saucepan over medium heat and bring the mixture to a simmer. Cook for 10 to 15 minutes, stirring occasionally, until peaches are tender and liquid has thickened slightly.

3. Remove pan from the heat and stir in the vanilla extract.

4. Place a waffle on a plate and spoon some of the peach cobbler topping over the waffle. Add a dollop of whipped cream or a scoop of vanilla ice cream, if desired. Serve immediately and enjoy!

For the waffles

- 1/2 cup milk
- 1/4 cup warm water
- 2 tablespoons light brown sugar
- 2 teaspoons active dry yeast
- 2 eggs
- 1 teaspoon vanilla extract
- 1/4 teaspoon salt
- 3 cups flour
- 14 tablespoons butter, softened, cut into small pieces
- 3/4 cup pearl sugar

For the topping

- 4–5 ripe peaches, peeled and sliced (if peaches are not in season, you can use 2 to 2 ½ cups of frozen peaches)
- 1/2 cup granulated sugar
- 1 teaspoon ground cinnamon
- 1/4 teaspoon ground nutmeg
- 1/4 cup unsalted butter
- 1 cup water
- 1 teaspoon vanilla extract
- Whipped cream or vanilla ice cream

CHEF'S TIP: Not ready to make your waffles? The dough can be left covered in the oil-sprayed bowl and refrigerated for use the next day.

DOUGLASS WILLIAMS

Douglass Williams's path to becoming one of the most celebrated chefs in the city has always fascinated us. Williams—known for his MIDA—grew up in Atlantic City. He was diagnosed with Crohn's disease at age sixteen, which meant that eating wasn't so easy.

Realizing that food was going to be a huge part of his health journey, Douglass learned how to make foods that were beneficial to the body—but also delicious. That led him to become a chef, and he found himself learning from some of the most well-known personalities in Boston.

After working in kitchens with mentors such as Michael Schlow, Christopher Myers, and Jamie Bissonette, he traveled the world for more education. Stops included Southeast Asia, Sardinia, New York City (at Michelin-starred Corton), and Paris (at Michelin-starred Akrame). Chef Williams then returned to Boston, ready to open MIDA in the South End in 2016.

Here's how we feel about Williams and MIDA: The minute you have his food, you'll know who he is for the *rest of your life*. It is no surprise that *Food & Wine* magazine put him on their list of the Top 10 Chefs in America. Or that Williams wound up opening two more MIDA locations, in Newton and East Boston. Menu staples include handmade pasta (like Bucatini All Amatriciana and Rock Shrimp Carbonara), entrees like Short Rib Lasagna, Eggplant Parmesan, and pizza.

That pizza is *so* good that he also opened APIZZA, a takeout and delivery spot in TD Garden's Hub Hall, specializing in New Haven– and Roman-style pie. Let's not forget D.W. French, the Parisian bistro near Fenway that belongs to Chef Williams too.

MIDA, by the way, comes from the Italian *mi da,* which means "he gives" or "she gives." A fitting name, because generosity is a pillar of Chef Williams's philosophy.

The night before Billy's son Chris got married, Chef Williams hosted the rehearsal dinner at MIDA in East Boston before it opened to the public. He accommodated everybody's dietary restrictions and had made a contingency plan just in case the city didn't give him his liquor license in time for the party. (That license did come through at the eleventh hour, and it was a party we'll never forget.)

The three-time James Beard semi-finalist and supporter of the No Kid Hungry organization has quickly become a leader in the Boston area, creating spaces that are warm and inclusive. He's a Black and Syrian Lebanese chef-owner who hangs LGBTQ pride flags as well as Black Lives Matter posters outside his restaurant. He makes guests know they are welcome. It's no surprise we often see big groups of friends laughing, enjoying themselves, and feeling at home at his establishments.

When Chef Williams isn't opening fantastic restaurants or traveling to find food experiences he can bring back to Boston, he and his lovely wife are raising their adorable twin boys, who are close in age to Jenny's daughters. Which reminds us, we should plan a playdate for the kids soon! (Billy can come, too.)

SHAKSHUKA

Serves 4

Shakshuka is a dish that has roots in North Africa and is a popular breakfast dish around the world. It is especially popular at MIDA when featured on their brunch menu.

1. In a cold pot (no heat), add the oil, garlic, onions, chili flakes, and 1 tablespoon each of salt and pepper.
2. Turn heat to high.
3. After 1 minute, all ingredients will begin to react with the increasingly hotter oil. Reduce heat to medium. Stir ingredients, being careful to keep them away from the sides of the pans so they cook evenly.
4. Let sweat for 5 minutes, then deglaze with vinegar.
5. Immediately add crushed tomatoes.
6. Turn the heat to medium high, give the mixture a stir, and taste for additional seasonings.
7. Once it comes to a complete simmer (even bubbles rolling gently along the entire surface, not just on one side of the pot) give another stir and taste and reduce the heat back to medium and let cook for 15 minutes.
8. Once 15 minutes have elapsed, pull the sauce from the stove and set aside.
9. Preheat broiler to high, using the middle rack.
10. Allow eggs to come to room temperature.
11. Place ricotta into a casserole dish in even dollops around the base.
12. Gently crack eggs into casserole dish, being careful to not break the yolks. They will roll and surround the ricotta, let them fall where they may.
13. Spoon 16 ounces of the prepared sauce into the casserole dish, some on top of the eggs, some in between. Be creative, but don't just "dump" the sauce into the dish, as you could break yolks and it's just an overall messy technique.
14. Gently sprinkle the shakshuka with a touch (about 4 pinches each) of salt and pepper and a drizzle of olive oil.
15. Place under the broiler for 5 minutes. You must keep an eye on this, as broiling can be tricky if you are not comfortable with the heat setting!

- 1 cup extra-virgin olive oil, plus more for drizzling
- 4 cloves garlic, smashed and rough chopped
- 1 small, yellow onion, diced small
- 2 pinches of chili flakes
- 1 tablespoon kosher salt, plus more to taste
- 1 tablespoon ground pepper, plus more to taste
- 1/4 cup red wine vinegar
- 1 (28-ounce) can crushed San Marzano tomatoes
- 8 ounces ricotta cheese
- 8 large eggs, room temperature
- 4 large pinches of chives or 2 scallions, thinly sliced for garnish
- 8 slices sourdough toast

You want there to be a slight char on the tomato sauce, some egg whites gently peeking though, and a faint gloss of olive oil coming to the top. Once you see this, pull the dish from the oven, take a small knife and look for an egg. Give a slight break to the yolk, if it is slightly runny and the white is completely cooked, that is perfect. On the other hand, if the white is still translucent, it needs another 2 to 4 minutes under the broiler.

16. When it's done to your satisfaction, pull from the oven and garnish with chives or scallions and a liberal drizzle of olive oil.

17. Place bread slices in a toaster or under the broiler. They should have the crispy level of breakfast toast, soft inside with a satisfying layer of crunch and seasoning on the outside.

18. Assemble your portions onto a place with a side of sourdough and voila!

> **Jenny:** Brunch at MIDA is so special. Chef Williams constantly works to fine tune his craft, and his passion for his artistry is evident in every bite of his food.
>
> **Billy:** He's a chef that always goes the extra mile.

Side Dish

SPOONFULS

Food is at the center of everything we do, serving as a mouthpiece of hospitality in Boston. While it's always important to us to showcase the opening of a new restaurant, it's been equally important to us to showcase organizations that are making sure everyone has access to healthy food. Thirty-eight percent of food produced in the US is uneaten or unsold. One in six households in Massachusetts are food insecure. Spoonfuls (formerly Lovin' Spoonfuls) bridges the gap between unsold, high-quality perishable food that would go to landfills and people and places that need it in Massachusetts.

Since 2010, founder and CEO Ashley Stanley and her highly trained staff have partnered with grocery stores, wholesalers, and farms to find a solution to food waste and help make our community healthier and more equitable. The non-profit's trucks load unsold fruits, vegetables, meat, and dairy and drive it to community organizations throughout the state that same day.

Stanley, who is a friend and supporter of everyone in the industry, is an incredible speaker whom we've loved interviewing and supporting for years. Because of her leadership and the hard work of her staff, they've been able to rescue thirty million pounds of food, which equals twenty-four million meals. In one year, they were able to provide over 375,000 people in the state with food to which they otherwise wouldn't have access.

Photo courtesy of Spoonfuls

Spoonfuls is close to our heart and to the hearts of many featured in this book who take part in their annual Ultimate Tailgate fundraiser. We're proud to highlight them, knowing every spoonful of effort and kindness helps feed our neighborhoods.

MATT KING

We first met Matt King when he was the newly appointed young executive chef at Stanhope Grill, then in the Jurys Boston Hotel. He admits to us now that he was nervous back then to do a TV interview with Billy. We find that hard to believe because he was great on camera—and because he'd already been cooking for superstars like Bono and Elton John in his former job in catering services at the Fleet Center (now TD Garden).

Now Chef King is the president and COO of Legal Sea Foods, a beloved and long-standing restaurant chain with twenty-seven locations and counting. We have a feeling those nerves are long gone!

Like with many chefs we've come to know and respect, Chef King's love of cooking began during his childhood. Growing up in Shrewsbury, his parents worked full-time jobs and came home late, often leaving the family to order takeout or go out to eat. But Chef King, who came across his mother's *Time Life Cookbook* series, decided to give cooking dinner a try.

He credits his grandfather, Benjamin Kreindel, a retired US Army Major, for fostering his love of cooking. His grandfather's travels introduced him to food from around the world, and he, in turn, introduced global cuisines to Matt.

Chef King has come a long way since the cookbooks of his childhood. He was the National Director of Culinary Development and Corporate Chef at Smith & Wollensky for many years before becoming the Vice President of Culinary at the steak restaurant empire. He even helped create a special knife for the restaurant's forty-fifth anniversary. (It's available for purchase for all you steak enthusiasts.)

It was through that job that he found his way to Legal Sea Foods and eventually earned the titles of president and COO.

We've always known Matt to care about sustainability, especially now as he works with purveyors whose philosophies align with his. He travels to bring flavors from different cities to Boston, is an avid marathon runner, and a proud father.

He gets the business, but he's still a chef at heart. Maybe that's why he was so excited to send us a recipe. We have a feeling his steak knives are always sharp and at the ready.

LOBSTER LATKES WITH HORSERADISH SOUR CREAM, POACHED EGGS, AND CAVIAR

Serves 10

Latkes are delicious potato fritters. Adding lobster and caviar to the mix gives them a chewier texture and more decadent flavor.

To make the horseradish sour cream

1. In a medium bowl, combine sour cream, horseradish, hot sauce, salt, and pepper. Mix well and refrigerate.

To make the lobster latkes

2. Crack eggs into another medium-size bowl and gently whisk.
3. Add onions, chives, potatoes, kosher salt, and black pepper.
4. Fold in the matzoh meal and let it sit for 20 minutes in the refrigerator.
5. Fold in the lobster meat.
6. Portion into 20 4-ounce cakes roughly 1/4 inch thick.
7. Preheat oven to 400°F.
8. Heat enough oil in a frying pan to shallow fry the cakes. Gently place cakes in the oil and brown on both sides. Place them on a paper towel–lined dish after frying as you work through the batch.
9. Transfer to a sheet pan and finish in the oven for 3 to 5 minutes to make sure potatoes are cooked in the center.

To make the poached eggs

1. Bring a mixture of water and white vinegar to a simmer (2 tablespoons vinegar per quart of water). Season with kosher salt.
2. Crack eggs individually into small portion cups.
3. Using a slotted spoon, stir the water to create a vortex and add the eggs as the water is spinning. The swirling helps prevent the "feathering" or long strands of egg from spreading.
4. Poach to desired doneness, roughly 5 minutes for a runny egg.

(Continued)

For the horseradish sour cream

- 1 cup sour cream
- 2 teaspoons prepared horseradish
- ⅛ teaspoon tabasco
- Kosher salt and black pepper, to taste

For the lobster latkes

- 2 eggs
- 1/2 cup peeled and grated white onions (about 1½ medium onions)
- 1/4 cup chopped chives
- 2 cups peeled and grated russet potatoes (about 2 large potatoes)
- 1 teaspoon kosher salt
- 1 teaspoon black pepper
- 1 cup matzoh meal
- 3/4 pounds lobster meat, roughly chopped
- Vegetable oil as needed for frying

For the poached eggs

- 1 quart water (more as needed)
- 2 tablespoons white vinegar (more as needed)
- 10 eggs (or however many you want to make)
- Kosher salt, to taste

To finish

1. Place 2 cooked latkes on a plate with 1 poached egg. Top with 2 teaspoons Horseradish Sour Cream and your favorite caviar (Chef King prefers Hackleback). Garnish with micro greens.

For the finish

⅓ ounces caviar

Micro greens for garnish

CHEF'S TIP: If you're not feeding a large crowd, latkes may be pan fried ahead of time, stored in the refrigerator, and then heated in an oven when needed, but they are best right out of the frying pan!

Jenny: I think it's safe to say, Matt King knows his turf AND surf.

Billy: He's King of the steak, and his knife skills are unparalleled.

MICHAEL SCHLOW

Not long ago, Michael Schlow opened his new Seamark Seafood & Cocktails and Old Wives' Tale speakeasy at the Encore Boston Harbor Hotel. The launch party boasted a red carpet packed with local and national celebrities, including model/actress Emily Ratajowski and Patriots legend Ty Law. That's because Chef Schlow knows how to launch something spectacular.

Every time he launches a new concept, he goes big. Foodies around the city hope for invites and wonder when they'll be able to book a table.

In reality, James Beard Award–winning Schlow is actually down-to-earth, despite all that flair and the fact he's appeared on shows from *Top Chef Masters* to *The Tonight Show with Jimmy Fallon*.

He's the kind of guy celebrities like because he *isn't* trying to be a big deal.

Hailing from Brooklyn, and spending his teenage years in New Jersey, Schlow's first restaurant job was as a dishwasher. He went on to work for many prestigious New York City restaurants; one of his greatest mentors was restaurateur Pino Luongo, who emphasized the importance of Tuscan cooking.

In 1995, Chef Schlow made his mark on Boston, breathing new life into Café Louis. But it was the opening of Radius in downtown Boston in 1999 that catapulted him into the spotlight.

Radius quickly garnered acclaim for its French-inspired modern cuisine, earning Chef Schlow the James Beard Award for Best Chef: Northeast.

Now, there's only one Billy who Jenny loves more than Billy Costa, and that's Billy Joel. Jenny has seen Billy Joel perform *twenty times*, named her daughter Vienna after the song, and Joel's music has been the soundtrack of Jenny's life. Michael Schlow happens to be friends with Billy Joel and is *well* aware of Jenny's love for the singer.

After many years of getting to know Jenny to make sure she was "cool," Chef Schlow texted Jenny one day to meet him at a restaurant at a certain time. When she arrived, there was Billy Joel—*the* Billy Joel!—enjoying dinner with his pal.

Jenny kept it together, trying to be as calm as Schlow is around celebrities.

Schlow and his menus are responsible for so many perfect memories around Boston, but that one, for Jenny, takes the cake.

MAINE CRAB TARTARE WITH CUCUMBER AND CILANTRO

Serves 2

A cool, flavorful, perfect breakfast to enjoy outside on a hot summer day. Adding Maine crab is the best way to enjoy this dish.

1. In a small mixing bowl, combine crabmeat, mayonnaise, thyme, chives, shallots, lemon juice, and olive oil. Season the crab mixture with salt and pepper.

2. In a second small mixing bowl, place the cucumbers with a bit of salt and the rice wine vinegar. Place both bowls in the refrigerator for at least 1 hour.

3. Spoon half the cucumbers into a 3-inch mold and place half the crabmeat on top of the cucumber. Pack slightly with the back of a spoon.

4. Remove the ring mold and garnish with cilantro. Repeat with the other half.

6 ounces jumbo lump crabmeat (cleaned)

1 tablespoon mayonnaise

1 pinch of fresh thyme

1 teaspoon fresh chives

1 tablespoon chopped shallots

Juice of half a lemon

2 tablespoons extra-virgin olive oil

4 tablespoons diced cucumber

1 tablespoon rice wine vinegar

2 pinches of micro cilantro (or regular, finely chopped)

Salt and pepper, to taste

CHEF'S TIP: If you do not have ring molds, you can improvise with a 3-inch cookie cutter.

ANTHONY CATURANO

It takes a lot of courage to open a restaurant *anywhere*, but it takes *real* chutzpah to open an Italian restaurant in Boston's historic North End neighborhood, where well-established Italian cuisine reigns supreme.

When Anthony Caturano opened Prezza twenty years ago, he was the young upstart, an unknown face on the scene. Quickly, though, he became a force in the neighborhood.

How did he do it? By presenting sumptuous dishes that won over locals. He wound up with a pack of regulars who kept coming back over, and over, and over again. Within a few years, Billy was devoted to Caturano's place and could often be found standing at the packed bar, sipping on a Ketel One Cosmo, shoulder to shoulder with other enthusiastic guests enjoying plates like handmade bucatini or grilled swordfish.

Caturano grew up in Revere and Danvers, part of an Italian family where he watched his mother and grandmother cook from the heart—making twice as much food as was needed. Prezza pays homage to his grandmother, named after her hometown in Italy's Abruzzo region, known for highlighting coastal and pastoral cuisine, by offering plates such as Grilled Branzino in a white wine butter sauce and olive tapenade, and Braised Short Rib Ravioli in Marsala.

A Taste of Boston

We've found that Chef Caturano is a man of action. Take for example, the fish. He wants the fish at his establishments to be as fresh as possible, so he became a skilled fisherman and became friendly with the well-known fishers in the area. When we filmed segments with him and he would prepare a recipe, we'd ask where the fish came from. He'd humbly say he caught the fish that morning off the pier, treating it very casually, as though any one of us could catch a giant fish if we really took a rod in our hands, woke up before the crack of dawn, did the research, and practiced.

With quiet confidence, he became the owner of the casual American restaurant Blue Ox in Lynn, and eventually opened Tonno Cucina e Cantina, a seafood-focused restaurant in Gloucester, where fish plates are taken *very* seriously. The menu boasts raw bar fare, Tuna Tartare, Spicy Octopus on a Bed of Sardinian Couscous, Handmade Orecchiette with Rabe and Sausage, and myriad other dishes that make the mouth water. A second location of Tonno has already opened in Wakefield.

We suspect Chef Caturano would say his favorite regulars are his two beautiful children, for whom he makes breakfast almost every morning.

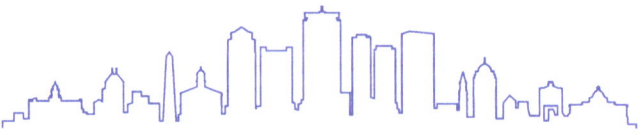

COTTAGE CHEESE PANCAKES

Serves 6 to 8

Fluffy and light as a cloud, these well-balanced pancakes are excellent fuel for each and every morning.

1. In a large bowl, mix the cottage cheese, eggs, and vanilla.
2. In another bowl whisk together the baking powder, sugar, and flour.
3. With a wooden spoon or spatula, slowly add the cottage cheese mixture to the dry ingredients until the ingredients come together, do not overmix.
4. Let sit for 15 minutes
5. The eggs and cottage cheese should provide enough liquid to make the batter. If not, a small amount of water or even whole milk can be used. The mixture should run a little and then stop.
6. Heat a large skillet or nonstick pan over medium high heat with some of the oil. There should be enough oil to coat the pan per batch.
7. Add the batter to the pan according to the size pancakes you can manage. Roughly a couple large spoonsful per pancake is what Chef Caturano usually does.
8. Once formed, sprinkle each pancake with the almonds if desired.
9. Chef suggests letting the first side really caramelize before flipping. Once the desired color is reached you can flip them. Be sure to lower the heat some if you add the almonds, as they will brown quicker than the first side.
10. Once done they can be plated with some fresh fruit, syrup, powdered sugar, or just eaten plain on the run.

1½ cups cottage cheese

4 eggs, lightly beaten

1 tablespoon vanilla extract

1 tablespoon baking powder

2 tablespoons sugar

1 cup flour

1/4 cup avocado oil, ghee, or other cooking oil

1 cup sliced almonds (optional)

1/2 cup fresh fruit (optional)

CHEF'S TIP: You can also substitute gluten-free flour in this recipe, but be sure to add a teaspoon of xanthum gum to help bind it.

JEN AND JOSH ZISKIN

There was a time when Tom Brady, one of the greatest athletes of all time, ate pasta. We don't know if he will come back around to eating certain foods, and we wish him well in his retirement.

But when his diet was less restricted in 2014, he said one of his favorite meals when out in Boston was the Tagliatelle al Ragu Bolognese from La Morra in Brookline. So really, one could say that the husband/wife restaurateur team of Jen and Josh Ziskin helped contribute to many Super Bowl wins.

The Ziskins are a very cool couple—and very local. Josh grew up in Brookline. Jen is from Plymouth. They met, worked together, eventually fell in love, and got married. Two days after their wedding they started working in La Morra, Italy. Josh was a chef there; Jen babysat for a well-known family in the wine business.

The experience was so important that when they were ready to launch a restaurant—with Josh as chef and Jen as wine director—they created a place that's a tribute to La Morra.

Their local La Morra just had its twentieth anniversary. Congratulations to all.

The couple still travel to Italy, constantly fine-tuning their craft, making sure guests are able to take part in what Jen and Josh learned and love about the region. They've also expanded their presence on Route 9 with another restaurant, Punch Bowl, a spacious modern tavern in a new hotel in Brookline. It features Josh's take on seasonal New England staples like Crispy Chicken Thigh Pot Pie and Pan-Roasted Hake, and features a wine and beverage list that prioritizes companies run by women. It's curated by Jen, who knows best.

The Ziskins not only support one another, but are able to support so many others in their communities. They have both been active with the Massachusetts Restaurant Association, volunteered their labor and resources to several non-profits and charities, and have always found ways to bring people together. When the pandemic hit, Jen became a leading member of Let's Talk Womxn, leading the Boston chapter in a national movement designed to help female-identified restaurateurs and entrepreneurs network and support one another.

We're always impressed by how they work as teammates. They are friends, spouses, and muses to each other. We love our spouses, but we're not sure what it would be like to work with them every day (love you, Rob and Michele). Good for the Ziskins, who've figured out how to partner in a way that benefits us all.

Even Tom Brady, when he was still eating carbs, at least.

The Ziskins may not have a Super Bowl ring, but to us they will always be champions.

SALT COD POTATO CAKES

Servers 10 to 12

A fresh take on a traditional fishcake, Chef Ziskin's Salt Cod Potato Cakes are deceptively simple, yet intricate and rich in taste.

1. Twenty-four hours before you're ready to prepare this recipe, start soaking your cod in a large amount of water. Change the water at least 3 times during that period.

2. When that is done, place all the ingredients into a small pot and place on low heat.

3. Bring to a simmer and cook until salt cod flakes apart, 20 to 30 minutes. Make sure the mixture never boils.

4. Strain the cod, reserving the liquid.

5. Boil potatoes in cold water, drain and mash.

6. Mix the cod with the mashed potatoes along with 1/2 cup of the cod cooking liquid.

7. Let cool, cover, and cool completely in the refrigerator.

8. When ready to cook, preheat the oven to 375°F.

9. Shape cod/potato mixture into 2½-inch patties, and flour.

10. Heat oil in a medium frying pan. Pan fry patties on both sides until golden brown.

11. Place in the oven for 8 to 10 minutes, until hot and ready to serve.

8 ounces salt cod, prepared
2 cups heavy cream
1/2 cup finely diced onion, about 1 small onion
Zest of 1 lemon
1 clove garlic, chopped
1 teaspoon chopped fresh thyme
1 pinch of chili flakes
5 medium Idaho potatoes, peeled and cut in four, about 2½ pounds
Flour for coating
Oil for frying

BOSTON CHILDREN'S MUSEUM

The iconic building with the giant milk bottle outside is the site of many a school field trip and a magical place that holds childhood memories of the past, present, and future. The Boston Children's Museum is a place meant for kids to learn from play. Since it was founded by Boston public school science teachers in 1913, it's the second oldest as well as one of the most important children's museums in the entire world.

The museum has three floors full of exhibits, such as a STEAM lab, Dinos in Space, Construction Zone, and PlaySpace. One of our favorite exhibits is the Japanese House, a home families can walk through that was gifted to the museum from Boston's sister city, Kyoto, Japan. The exhibits bring forward the museum's mission of having children and families experience learning as an adventure and to keep their childhood curiosity and imagination throughout their lives.

This sense of play is really contagious. Billy got a little too into the spirit of the museum during one of our shoots there for our old show TV Diner. He, probably trying to have as much fun as the kids and wanting to show them a good time, decided to try what looked to be a high kick and somersault combination. Unfortunately, he landed on his shoulder in a not-so-fun way, and we had to go to the hospital. The staff at the Boston Children's Museum were very helpful, and we chalked it up to the museum's power of play.

MICHAEL LOMBARDI

We've noticed that many of our favorite chefs found inspiration when they were kids. Michael Lombardi, chef/owner of SRV in the South End and Si Cara in Cambridge, is a perfect example.

The New Haven, Connecticut, native grew up in an Italian American family where cooking meals for loved ones was important and a part of everyday life. When the kids in his family asked his grandparents for a snack or special dish, they would sweetly respond, "Si, Cara" meaning "Yes, Dear" in Italian, and provide.

It was around that time, by the way, that Lombardi would have been sitting alone in his living room watching Emeril Lagasse on TV. The Fall River chef made himself a star by cooking with a showmanship that impressed Lombardi.

Maybe that's why, after getting a degree from Boston University's School of Management, Lombardi wound up enrolling at The Culinary Institute of America. From there, he moved to Orvieto, Italy, to be mentored by Chef Lorenzo Polegri. After years of education and travel, Lombardi teamed up with friends to open a new Italian restaurant in Boston.

If you're a local foodie, you probably know it—SRV. You might not know that it stands for Serene Republic of Venice.

SRV was a James Beard semi-finalist for Best New Restaurant, and it is easy to see why. For us, it's the out-of-this-world risotto. But it's also SRV's vibe. SRV brought the *bacaro* (Venetian bar) experience to the South End. Before Chef Lombardi's restaurant showed up, neighbors would walk to Tremont Street to have a nice meal out. SRV changed all that, becoming a go-to destination for people in the neighborhood and *well* beyond. (It also created a new corner for cuisine, right at Mass Ave. and Columbus.)

Guests can enjoy a seasonally changing menu of Venetian delicacies that includes *cicchetti* (small bites) such as *polpette* (meatballs), main courses such as Squid Ink Risotto, and *dolci* (dessert) such as tiramisu. Or they can just pop in for an *ombra* (small glass of wine), or exceptional cocktails, like an Aperol Spritz, made by kind and knowledgeable bartenders.

In 2022 Chef Lombardi opened the casual yet gourmet Si Cara in the Central Square area of Cambridge. Specializing in New Age Neapolitan Canotto-style pizza, Si Cara pays loving tribute to Michael's grandparents' generosity when he was growing up. He does that with a toppings twist (leek kimchi on pizza? Yes, please!).

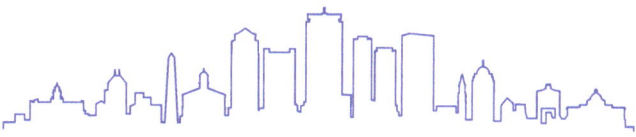

BACON POTATO GRUYÈRE PIZZA

Makes 2 10- to 12-inch pizzas

Pizza at breakfast? With this inventive recipe, pizza is great anytime, especially when the crust is so pillowy soft.

To make the pizza dough

Dough should be made 24 hours before you want to use it.

1. In a bowl, mix all ingredients together and knead the dough until it is smooth to the touch. Cover in plastic wrap and leave the bowl on the counter for 90 minutes. Then transfer the dough to the refrigerator for 24 hours.

2. Two to three hours before you are ready to use the dough, remove it from the refrigerator and divide it into two equal balls. Roll them on the counter until they are smooth with no seams on the bottom. Allow it to proof on the counter until it is doubled in size. (Time may vary depending on the temperature of the day.)

To make the pizza topping

1. Place bacon into medium-size pot over medium-high heat. When bacon starts to render a little bit of fat, add onions and potatoes.

2. Gently stir, allowing the bacon to get some color and the onions and potato to become soft. You shouldn't need to add salt because of the bacon, but taste it and adjust the mix if needed. Strain off the fat and cool the bacon mixture in the refrigerator.

To make the pizza sauce

Place all of the ingredients in a blender and blend until smooth.

To make the salsa verde

Mix all of the ingredients together in a bowl.

To make the poached eggs

1. Bring water to a strong simmer. Add white vinegar. With a whisk, make a whirlpool with the simmering water and crack the eggs into the center of the vortex. Only do as many eggs at a time as you feel comfortable with. The eggs should slightly drop the temperature of the water, losing the simmer. If it is still making bubbles on top of the water, slightly lower the temperature until the water is hot but not bubbling.

(Continued)

2 ½-pound pizza dough balls

For the pizza dough (if you want to make it instead of buying it)

This is a 24-hour process.

2⅓ cups caputo pizza flour

1 tablespoon room-temperature water

1 teaspoon salt

1/4 teaspoon active dry yeast

For the pizza topping

4 slices bacon, cut into 1/2-inch strips

1 medium red onion, cut into 1/2-inch strips

1 Idaho potato, sliced thin with mandoline or side of a box grater

Salt, to taste

1 cup shredded gruyère cheese

For the pizza sauce

1 8-ounce can unseasoned chopped or diced tomato

1/2 clove garlic, raw

1 teaspoon dried oregano

1 teaspoon kosher salt

2. Leave the eggs untouched for 3 minutes, then check them with a slotted spoon. The eggs shouldn't move quite as much and the white should feel firm and hold its shape.

3. Move them to a plate lined with a towel to remove the excess water. Transfer them to a plate and store until you need them (they can be held in the refrigerator)

To make the pizzas

1. Preheat oven to 500°F. If you have pizza stone, move it to the top rack in your oven. Allow the stone to sit in the 500°F oven for 30 minutes before baking your first pizza. If you don't have a stone, you can shape the pizza and bake it in a large cast-iron pan (lightly oiled) or you can bake the pizza on a baking sheet.

2. Make sure your dough is soft to the touch and room temperature. It should be double in size from when it started. Working from the center of the dough, push your fingers down, working out to the edge of the pizza. Leave a small lip for the crust. Then working with your palms flat and in the middle of the dough, stretch the dough larger and larger until you have the size circle you desire. A 1/2-pound dough ball should make a 10- to 12-inch pizza. You will do this with both dough balls.

3. Spoon 3 ounces of pizza sauce into the middle of each dough and spread it evenly, allowing the crust to remain untouched.

4. Place the pizzas, one at a time, onto a peel and load it into your oven. Bake for about 8 minutes each.

5. Remove pizza from the oven (the crust should be set but not fully browned and cooked) and once both pizzas are cooked, spread the bacon, potato, onion mix evenly across each pizza. Top everything with the shredded gruyère.

6. Place the pizzas back in the oven for 4 to 5 more minutes each.

7. Take the pizzas out, place 4 poached eggs onto each, and place them back into the oven for about 2 minutes or until the crust is fully browned, the cheese and toppings are melted, and the poached eggs are warm but the yolk is still runny. Depending on how efficient the oven is, these times might be a bit longer or shorter.

8. Remove the pizza from the oven and cut it into 4 slices, with a poached egg on each slice.

9. Season the eggs with cracked black pepper and sea salt. Drizzle the parsley mixture around the pizza and enjoy!

For the salsa verde

1/2 cup chopped parsley

1 teaspoon crushed red pepper (more if you want it spicier)

1 teaspoon lemon juice

1/4 cup olive oil

Pinch of salt

For the poached eggs

8 eggs

4 quarts water

1/4 cup white vinegar

JEREMY SEWALL

We're convinced Jeremy Sewall can speak to the sea. Maybe that's because his connection to the ocean began way before he was born.

Sewall—of Row 34 fame—comes from a long lineage of lobstermen and fisherman. His grandfather was one of the original lobstermen out of York Harbor in Maine during the 1930s. Growing up, Chef Sewall would visit his family in Maine every summer, joining relatives on boats, catching fish and lobster, and enjoying the day's catch at family cookouts.

Years later, after graduating from The Culinary Institute of America, he worked as a chef at the White Barn Inn in Kennebunkport, went abroad to learn more about his craft, worked for some of the most prominent restaurants in Boston, including L'Espalier, where he met his wonderful wife Lisa who worked there as a pastry chef.

He became a restaurateur with Lineage, Sewall and Lisa's elegant spot for modern American cuisine in Brookline, followed by a partnership with Shore Gregory, in the beloved Island Creek Oyster Bar.

Then came Row 34 in Fort Point, where Sewall not only serves some of the tastiest, gorgeous local seafood in the city, but also offers a scene where friends gather after work, celebrating over ceviche, choosing from a menu of oysters, and feeling as if they're getting the best New England has to offer.

A Taste of Boston

It's no surprise that there are now four locations of Row 34. Lucky residents in Cambridge, Burlington, and Portsmouth, New Hampshire, now have branches, with Sewall as captain. Over the years, the captain and his restaurant teams have raised a lot of money and awareness for Friends of Dana Farber, a non-profit near to their hearts.

Chef Sewall is also the co-author of three excellent cookbooks, one of which was nominated for a James Beard Award.

We're honored he saved one recipe for us. This one comes from home, because when he's with Lisa and their three wonderful kids, he loves to focus on the first meal of the day.

> **Billy:** Poached eggs at home. Fancy!
>
> **Jenny:** Can you poach an egg, Billy?
>
> **Billy:** With Chef Sewall's guidance, I just might be able to.

POACHED EGGS WITH PROSCIUTTO, ARUGULA, TOMATOES, AND SALSA VERDE

Serves 2

Fresh arugula, tomatoes, and vegetables from a farm or CSA are preferred for this breakfast full of eye-popping color.

To make the salsa verde

1. Place everything but the salt and pepper in a food processor or use a hand blender to puree smooth.
2. Taste and season with salt and pepper as needed.
3. Keep cold until ready to use.

To make the poached eggs, prosciutto, arugula, and tomatoes

1. In a large pot, combine vinegar and 3 cups water and bring to a simmer.
2. While the water is warming, brush sourdough slices with olive oil and toast lightly on the stovetop (or in the oven) on both sides.
3. Put toasted sourdough on serving plates and begin to layer the other ingredients, starting with the arugula followed by the prosciutto, avocado, and finally the sliced tomato. Season with salt and pepper as you layer the avocado and tomato.
4. Carefully crack the eggs and drop into the water to poach for 3 minutes. Carefully remove with a slotted spoon and let drain. Place an egg on top of the tomatoes on each slice of sourdough.
5. Top each egg with the salsa verde.

For the salsa verde

- 1/2 cup Italian parsley leaves
- 1/2 cup basil leaves
- 1/4 cup cilantro leaves
- 6 mint leaves
- 1 small clove garlic
- 1 teaspoon lemon zest
- 1 tablespoon lemon juice
- 1 teaspoon Dijon mustard
- 10 capers
- 1/4 teaspoon chili flakes
- 1/2 cup extra-virgin olive oil
- Salt and pepper, to taste

For the poached eggs, prosciutto, arugula, and tomatoes

- 2 tablespoons distilled vinegar
- 2 slices sourdough bread
- 2 tablespoons extra-virgin olive oil
- 1/2 cup arugula leaves
- 6 slices prosciutto
- 1 ripe avocado, peeled and pitted, sliced thin
- 1 red beefsteak tomato, cored and sliced thin
- Salt and pepper, to taste
- 2 large whole eggs

DEBORAH HANSEN

It takes a lot of passion—and perseverance—to open a restaurant. It takes something else to keep a restaurant running for more than twenty-five years.

Taberna de Haro, a slice of Spain in Brookline, is as perfect as it was when it opened. That's why it is a neighborhood staple, adored by longtime customers and people who have the pleasure of discovering it for the first time.

Credit goes to Chef/owner/sommelier Deborah Hansen who's been passionate about Spanish culture and cuisine since she was an undergrad at Bates College studying abroad in Madrid. That's where Hansen earned her master's degree from New York University abroad, where she earned her sommelier title, where she first opened a restaurant, and where her two beautiful daughters were born.

When she came back to the states in the late 1990s, she wanted to bring authentic Spanish cuisine to Boston. Not just Americanized versions of Spanish food, but the real-deal flavors, scents, ingredients, and wine she fell in love with.

Her take on a true Spanish experience is a warm and cozy dining room that welcomes you with Albondigas (Madrid-style meatballs), Arroz Negro (squid ink, squid, saffron paella), and Patatas Riojanas (local golden potatoes braised with red and green peppers, chorizo, garlic, pimentón, and wine).

The menu changes with the season, and in the summer, the patio is open for guests to relax, enjoy, and share tapas such as Bunuelos de Dacalo (saffron–salt cod balls), anchovies and olives imported from Spain, and Berberechos al Limon (cockles with white wine, garlic, and lemon). No matter what's on the menu, Chef Hansen uses local and in-season produce. The olive oil is always from Spain and always on hand.

Also imported from Spain is Hansen's comprehensive wine list with more than three hundred options. Taberna de Haro has won a slew of wine awards over the years, including Wine Spectator's Award of Excellence, which the restaurant has received annually since 2004.

What we've always appreciated is that Deborah makes the wine list accessible. There's nothing intimidating about the experience—thanks to her knowledge and kindness.

Whether a guest is ordering an affordable bottle of wine or wants a more elite experience, she wants guests to explore, have fun, and learn something new. She and her dedicated staff, who have trainings/tastings under Sommelier Hansen's instruction, know exactly how to advise on pairings.

Getting to Spain isn't always easy, but we are lucky—and grateful—that Deborah Hansen has brought it so close to home.

LEMON OLIVE OIL CAKE

Serves 8

This moist pound cake uses olive oil instead of butter and hits like a burst of Spanish sunshine. Use it for brunches, as you can bake it the day before; serve it as a lovely desert in the summer topped with fresh fruit; enjoy it with tea on a wintry afternoon with jam; or have it for breakfast with some ricotta cheese (requesón in Spanish) and a coffee. As easy and versatile as it is delicious!

1. Preheat oven to 350ºF.

2. Oil and flour a 9-inch cake pan, knocking out excess flour. (1 teaspoon butter works a bit better than the oil if you don't need the cake to be dairy-free.)

3. In a food processor or blender, beat the fruit zest, juice (you should have about 1/3 cup juice), eggs, oil, and sugar for 5 minutes. Feel free to whisk by hand in a big bowl if you are feeling energetic.

4. Sift the flour, baking powder, and salt in a large mixing bowl.

5. Pour the oil mixture into the dry mixture and stir with a rubber spatula until smooth and no trace of flour is visible. (Don't mix in the blender, as this will toughen your cake).

6. Pour the batter into the prepared pan and place in the center of the oven. Reduce heat to 325ºF and bake for 1 hour and 15 minutes.

7. If your oven is particularly hot and efficient, your cake may be done in 1 hour. Open the oven door the tiniest crack to peek, as you don't want to let the heat out. The cake should be raised in the center, pulling away from the sides of the pan, and be a rich golden brown in color.

8. Cool on a rack for 10 minutes before removing from pan. Try to wait 10 more minutes before cutting.

- 1 lemon, zested and juiced
- 1 orange, zested and juiced
- 4 eggs
- 1 cup extra-virgin Spanish olive oil, best quality, plus 1 teaspoon for the pan
- 1 cup sugar
- 1 cup flour, plus 1 teaspoon for the pan
- 1 tablespoon baking powder
- 1 pinch of salt

TOM BERRY

Some signs you're at a Tom Berry establishment, under his Coje Management Group: 1. There are very hip twenty-somethings lined up outside. 2. You feel the *energy*—like you're at the coolest party in town. 3. The decor is unforgettable—from winding bamboo that makes the inside of the restaurant feel like an otherworldly paradise, to a ceiling that makes you feel like you're in a French bistro in another time. 4. You're enjoying internationally inspired fusion dishes you can't get anywhere else—because every Coje restaurant offers a singular experience that can't be replicated.

Thank you, Coje and Chef Berry, for bringing Coquette, Mariel, Yvonne's, RUKA, Underground, and Caveau into our lives.

Despite the international vibe of Chef Berry's concepts, he's actually a local guy. Chef Berry grew up in New Hampshire, and his first taste of life as a chef came when he was thirteen years old. He asked his mother to help him cook a lemon Dijon chicken from a recipe he found on the cover of *Bon Appetit* magazine. When he served the chicken to all the neighborhood kids and saw how much they loved it, he caught the chef bug.

After graduating from Johnson & Wales University, he began his career at Ming Tsai's Blue Ginger in Wellesley. He then spread his wings with executive chef positions at Bambara in the Hotel Marlowe and later at Temple Bar in Cambridge.

Now at Coje, he helms a brand of restaurants that are some of the most popular in the city and specialize in being lavish, eccentric, and vibrant. They inundate guests with unique food and experiences that have young tastemakers coming back for more and hashtagging to their hearts' delight.

At Lolita Cocina & Tequila Bar in Back Bay and Fort Point, Mexican food is made modern with tuna tostadas and spicy Brussels sprout tacos, served with out-of-this-world margaritas. The meal is topped off with overflowing, complimentary cotton candy. Over at the swoony Coquette in the Omni Seaport Hotel, French and Mediterranean food finds a charming blend in a space that is an artistic feast for the eyes. RUKA, meanwhile, is a blend of Peruvian and Asian flavors in a restaurant space that looks like an otherworldly paradise—right in the middle of Downtown Crossing.

To Chef Berry, we find ourselves saying, "Thank you for keeping Boston so cool."

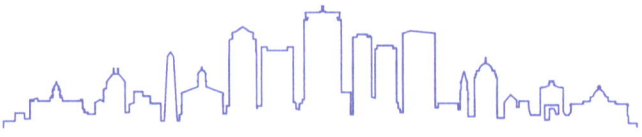

MULBERRY FRENCH TOAST

Serves 4

Portugese sweet bread, pistachio labneh, mulberry maple syrup, berries, and toasted pistachios make this your new favorite way to have French toast.

To make the pistachio labneh

1. Mix ingredients in a bowl, allow to rest for a few hours in the fridge, overnight is better.

To make the mulberry maple syrup

1. Puree all ingredients in blender. This can be stored in the fridge for up to a week. Warm gently before serving.

To make the French toast batter

In a medium bowl, whisk all the ingredients until incorporated.

To make the French toast

1. Preheat large, nonstick skillet over medium-low heat.

2. Soak the bread slices in the batter just before cooking, for about 1 minute.

3. Melt butter in the pan and add the soaked sliced bread. Cook until very golden and cooked through, 3 to 4 minutes per side.

To finish

1. Arrange two slices of French toast on each plate.

2. Drizzle about 1/3 cup of mulberry molasses over each order, and top with 1/4 cup of pistachio labneh.

3. Evenly divide the crushed pistachios, blueberries, and strawberries over the top, garnish with a dusting of powdered sugar.

NOTE: Mulberry jam and syrup, as well as pistachio paste, can be found in specialty grocery stores or online.

For the pistachio labneh

- 1 cup labneh (cow's milk)
- 1 tablespoon pistachio praline paste (or nut butter)
- 1/8 teaspoon salt
- 1/8 teaspoon vanilla paste (substitue: vanilla extract)

For mulberry maple syrup

- 1 cup pure maple syrup
- 1/4 cup mulberry molasses/syrup
- 1/4 cup seeded mulberry jam
- 1/2 teaspoon salt

For the French toast batter

- 8 large eggs
- 1/2 cup heavy cream
- 1 teaspoon pumpkin pie spice
- 1 teaspoon vanilla extract
- 1/2 teaspoon salt
- 1/2 teaspoon granulated sugar

For the French toast

- 8 1-inch-thick slices day-old Portuguese sweet bread
- 1–2 tablespoons unsalted butter for cooking

For the finish

- 1/2 cup roasted, unsalted pistachios, gently crushed
- 1/2 cup fresh blueberries
- 1/2 cup sliced strawberries
- Powdered sugar for dusting

MARK CINA AND TOM SCHLESINGER-GUIDELLI

*G*o through a magic archway not far from TD Garden, and you'll come upon Alcove, a lovely restaurant by the water and an oasis from the action near the North End.

That's where we go for delicious meals with a view of sailboats and city skyline. It's where we eat some of our favorite dishes, such as Monkfish Milanese, Halibut Ceviche, and Arugula and Chicory Salad.

Alcove is run by two veterans in the local food scene—Tom Schlesinger-Guidelli, who has worked with the best of the best, and Chef Mark Cina, a seasoned pro from his time helming prestigious East and West Coast kitchens.

Their Seaport venture, Hook + Line, serves a modern spin on New England seafood classics, and guests are happy to be reeled in.

We first met Tom when he was cutting his teeth at his uncle Chef Chris Schlesinger's East Coast Grill in Cambridge. Tom had grown up in the restaurant industry working at his uncle's restaurants, and when your uncle is a James Beard Award–winning chef, there's *a lot* to learn. And so, he did, but not just about what goes on in a kitchen. Tom went to Kenyon College, thinking he'd never get back into the family business and would go into politics or archaeology. But after a trip to an archaeological dig site in Honduras, he found all he really wanted to do was read about wine.

A Taste of Boston

Tom came home, worked at the bar in Garrett Harker's Eastern Standard Kitchen, getting an education on wine and cocktails that lead him to become the bar manager at Tony Maw's Craigie on Main. We had Tom on our program during his time at Craigie to show us how to mix some great cocktails. He was polished, playful, educated, and could tell us more about wine and spirits than anyone in the city, but he always made his lessons approachable and fun.

It would have made sense for Tom to stay on the mixology and wine track, as he was quickly winning accolades, but he changed course, becoming the opening general manager of Island Creek Oyster Bar, working again with Garrett Harker. After consulting for restaurants like Pagu and The Automatic, Tom felt he was ready to open his own restaurant.

Alcove, Tom's neighborhood ode to the farm coast of New England, is tucked away in Boston's West End near TD Garden and overlooks the harbor. It's a lively spot for guests to have a meal before or after a concert or a Bruins or Celtics game.

But the food and atmosphere keep people coming even when there isn't an event at the Garden. (Jenny hosted her sister's baby shower at Alcove, which was an event in and of itself!) With a raw bar, a seasonally changing menu featuring the bounty of the land and sea, and a cocktail menu full of flourish, Alcove proved that Tom was on the right track. He wanted to open another restaurant and knew he needed a chef. As luck would have it, Chef Mark Cina was nearby on Nantucket.

The gregarious Chef Cina grew up in Needham and Cape Cod and had worked in kitchens in Boston, including Craigie Street Bistrot and Susan Regis's Upstairs at the Pudding. He spent many years on the West Coast at restaurants like Daniel Patterson's Alta before returning to Boston and leading the kitchen at Yvonne's Supper Club. After backpacking and cooking his way through Europe, Chef Cina was in Nantucket at Chef Gabriel Frasca's Straight Wharf when he heard Tom Schlesinger-Guidelli was looking for a chef.

Hook + Line and H+L Market are the duo's way of paying homage to the New England seafood they grew up eating while also creatively expanding how seafood should be enjoyed. Hook + Line is by the waterfront and has a gorgeous seasonal patio as well as a lush indoor dining area for 275 guests. They have a giant raw bar, clam chowder, stuffies, lobster rolls, and fried clams; but they also utilize a giant wood-fired grill to serve wood-grilled cuttlefish, yellowfin tuna steak, tiger prawns, and even steak or chicken if you're feeling more turf than surf.

The two have created a dining experience that is upscale yet approachable, and we can tell they're having as much fun in the restaurant as their guests are.

SMOKED HAM GRITS BENEDICT

Serves 2

This is a benedict with smoked ham grits, slow-roasted tomato, poached eggs, and hollandaise. The grits are delicious on the toasted English muffin (or by themselves), and the slow-roasted tomato acts as a cup to hold the poached egg. The ham hock takes some time to braise, as do the tomatoes to slow roast (which intensifies their flavor), but your patience will turn into deliciousness.

To make the hollandaise
1. Put everything except the butter in a blender and puree.
2. Stream in the butter to emulsify. Keep warm, but not hot.

To make the ham
1. Add the ham hock and chicken stock to a 4-quart pan. Cover and cook at a low simmer until the meat is very tender, about 1 hour. Try not to reduce the liquid too much during cooking.
2. When the ham hocks are tender, let them cool in the broth, then pull out and pick the meat into small pieces.

To make the tomatoes
1. Preheat the oven to 300°F.
2. Cut tomatoes in half lengthwise and scoop out the insides (reserve for another use). Toss the tomatoes gently with olive oil, salt, and pepper, and place on a wire rack over a sheet pan so the tomatoes get air circulation. Cook until half dried and slightly brown around the edges, about 35 minutes.

To make the grits
1. In a 1- to 2-quart sauce pot, gently sweat the onion and thyme in butter and a few drops of water until soft. Season with salt as you go.
2. Add 1 cup of the liquid you braised the ham hock in.
3. Add in milk and cream.
4. Bring this all to a simmer, then whisk in the grits. Reduce to medium-low heat, and stir often while they cook, 5 to 7 minutes.
5. Once grits are cooked, fold in the cheese and about a 1/2 cup of the braised ham hock meat.

For the hollandaise
1½ egg yolks
2 teaspoons champagne vinegar
1/2 teaspoon lemon juice
2 drops of tabasco
4 teaspoons warm water
Pinch of salt
3/4 cup brown butter, melted

For the ham
1 smoked ham hock
3 quarts chicken stock

For the tomatoes
2 roma tomatoes
1–2 tablespoons olive oil
Salt, to taste
Black pepper, to taste

For the grits
1 tablespoon finely diced Spanish onion
Leaves from 2 sprigs of thyme
1 ounce butter
1½ cups milk
1/2 cup heavy cream
1/2 cup instant grits
1/2 cup cheddar cheese
Fresh black pepper
3 tablespoons finely sliced chives, optional

For the finish
2 English muffins
4 eggs
Sea salt, to taste

6. Add a few cracks of fresh black pepper. I like to fold in finely sliced chives as well.

To finish

1. While the grits cook, butter and griddle your English muffins to perfection.

2. Meanwhile, bring a small pot of lightly salted water to a bare simmer for the eggs.

3. When everything else is close to done, drop your 4 eggs into the water to poach, cooking them 3 to 4 minutes depending on how you like them done.

4. Scoop 2 to 3 tablespoons of smoked ham grits onto your buttered English muffins.

5. Place a roasted tomato, cut-side-up on top of the grits. This will hold the poached egg snugly.

6. Gently place the egg onto the tomato, drop a few granules of flaky sea salt on them and top with hollandaise sauce.

7. Enjoy!

MARC ORFALY

One of us *really* loves boats—loves being on a boat, loves talking about boats, waits all year for the New England boat show, and can parallel park his boat at the Charlestown Marina dock like a boss.

So, when the Navy Yard Hospitality Group came on the scene with their gorgeous nautically themed waterfront restaurants, Captain Costa—yes, the boat lover here is Billy—was thrilled he'd have more favorite spots to set anchor in the summer. Pier 6 in Boston's Navy Yard; ReelHouse in East Boston, Marina Bay, and the Seaport; and the Tall Ship, a literal 245-foot Canadian tall ship that was brought to East Boston and turned into a magnificent floating oyster bar.

The Navy Yard Hospitality Group is captained by restaurateur Charlie Larner. His mission? To revitalize the city's waterfront properties and create spaces for people to enjoy the views with amazing food, drinks, and service. As any good captain or restaurateur knows, you need someone to helm the ship or restaurant. Enter seven-time James Beard–nominated chef, Marc Orfaly, the culinary director extraordinaire of the Navy Yard Hospitality Group.

Chef Orfaly grew up in Brookline and worked in impressive restaurant kitchens along the East and West Coasts. But it was the opening of his own Parisian bistro Pigalle in 2001 that really caught the city of Boston's attention. *Esquire* magazine named him "One of the Top Chefs to Watch in the Country," and we have been watching. We've watched his expertise grow as he took on executive chef duties at Beehive; opened the Italian restaurant Marco in the North End; worked with Peking Tom's, Remick's, and Summer House; and garnered acclaim and awards in his thirty years of being a great chef. Now we've seen how he can change the entire scope of a waterfront. We also love to watch as his menus grow. At ReelHouse, for instance, there's a raw bar complete with shellfish towers and New England seafood staples like lobster rolls, but there are also offerings like Crab Fried Rice, Shrimp Fra Diavlo, and Elote Corn "Off the Cob."

Those are some of the dishes that have Billy docking there year after year.

TIPICO MONTANERO

Serves 4 to 6

Tipico Montanero is a typical plate found in Medellin, Colombia, full of the region's staples. It can serve as a hearty breakfast and is awesome for a savory brunch.

To make the rice

1. Put rice in a fine mesh strainer and rinse with cold water. Transfer to a pot with the water and salt. Bring to a boil and simmer until done, about 15 minutes. Alternatively, use a rice cooker.

To make the beans

1. Preheat oven to 325°F.
2. Heat oil in a Dutch oven over medium heat.
3. Sauté onion, garlic, and peppers until tender.
4. Add spices and tomato paste, and toast for 20 seconds to release all aromatics.
5. Add the rinsed red kidney beans that have soaked overnight.
6. Pour in veal stock and bring to a boil. Cover with aluminum foil and add the pot cover to seal it properly.
7. Place in the oven and bake until tender, about 1 hour, checking after 45 minutes. Depending on the age of the beans it might take longer. Add more stock if necessary.

To make the poached egg

1. Bring water to a boil and add vinegar.
2. Drop freshly cracked egg in and cook 2 to 3 minutes depending on the size of the egg and your preference.

To make the chicharron

1. Cook bacon in the oven at 400°F for 20 to 30 minutes or deep fry. Oven baked chicharrón will get more rendered without adding much color, while deep-fried will get crunchier and add more color.

To make the shishito peppers

1. Mix peppers with olive oil, and sauté in a hot pan until they are blistered, about 12 minutes. Alternately, these peppers can be grilled.

To finish

Serve with grilled sirloin tips and a house salad (both optional).

For the rice

- 1 cup jasmine rice
- 2 cups water
- Salt, to taste

For the beans

- 3 tablespoons canola oil
- 1 small white onion, finely chopped
- 3 garlic cloves, chopped
- 1 red pepper, diced
- 1 yellow pepper, diced
- 2 teaspoons ground cumin
- 2 teaspoons paprika
- 1 teaspoon chili powder
- 1 tablespoon tomato paste
- 2 cups red kidney bean (pre-soaked overnight)
- 6 cups veal stock
- Salt, to taste

For the poached egg

- 1 quart water
- 2 tablespoons white vinegar

For the chicharron

- 1/2 pound bacon, thick cut and scored

For the shishito peppers

- 2 cups whole shishito peppers
- 2 tablespoons olive oil

Side Dish

BOSTON YACHT HAVEN INN & MARINA

For years, we felt the Boston Yacht Haven Inn, a luxury ten-room boutique inn on the Commercial Wharf with decks and a giant outdoor patio overlooking the harbor, was one of the best kept secrets for a staycation or for people visiting the city.

The secret is out, with guests raving about the views of Boston from the inn's private balconies, being able to wake up and watch the ships sail by, the exceptional service, the food, the proximity to city attractions, the water taxis that can take you wherever you want to go, and learning that one doesn't have to have a boat in the Yacht Haven Marina to stay at the inn. Though, as Billy can attest, there's nothing better than being on a boat, and one of the most special places to him is the Boston Yacht Haven Inn.

When Billy brought Michele to the inn, she knew if they ever got married, they had to have the wedding there. When Billy asked the owners if this was possible, they said they'd never held a wedding, but there's a first time for everything! Billy and Michele had their beautiful wedding at the nautical and wondrous inn. With all ten

Photo by Michael Blanchard

rooms booked, amazing food from the inn's Chef Rene, and the couple's dog, Bessie, serving as flower girl, everyone at the wedding had a ball. It's Billy and Michele's magic place. If you need a little magic in your life, set your sails for the Boston Yacht Haven Inn.

Lunch

TIFFANI FAISON

We've known a lot of brilliant chefs who are introverts. Many prefer to shine in the kitchen, out of the limelight. Tiffani Faison is *not on that list*.

Chef Faison is a talented, creative, winning chef who is excellent on camera. It's no surprise to us; her food is always spectacular, but her presence is always felt, as is her star quality.

In 2007 we were doing a segment at Michela Larson's Rocca, and as Chef Tiffani Faison walked out of the kitchen, we felt her energy before we even saw her face. Her aura, her vibrant red hair, her storytelling ability, her skills as a chef—all of this had us thinking *What a dynamo*. Later, when she became a must-watch personality on *Top Chef*, we thought, *Of course*! The James Beard nominee is a major talent in the culinary scene, but she also happens to be the coolest lady in the room.

A self-proclaimed army kid, Chef Faison moved around the US throughout her childhood. She experienced regional cuisines and realized how much flavor there is right in our country. With her Big Heart Hospitality Group restaurants, she brings her travels to her menus.

With Sweet Cheeks Q in Fenway, you can enjoy Southern barbecue without having to take a trip to Texas. At Dive Bar, not only can you find New England lobster rolls but New Orleans–style shrimp po'boys and other seafood favorites. At Bubble Bath, adults can delight in having white sturgeon caviar over Lay's potato chips, lathered in sour cream and chives, while sipping on champagne. If you're in the mood for kick-ass cocktails and snacks, head over to Fool's Errand. And if you miss the '70s and '80s, Tenderoni's Pizza is the perfect blend of nostalgia and razzle-dazzle, tapping into childhood faves and elevating them for adult palates.

Tiffani is not only creative, she's fearless. She comes up with exciting and fun dining concepts and follows up on them no matter what anybody thinks. She's never backed down from a challenge, and this is also true of when she's on TV. As the runner-up on the first season of *Top Chef*, she became a star and continued to wow audiences on programs like *Chopped*, *Tournament of Champions* (which she won and has a huge World Wrestling–style belt to prove it), *Beachside Brawl*, *Beat Bobby Flay*, *Guy's Grocery Games*, and so many national and local talk shows that we're pretty sure Tiffani could host her own show if she wanted to.

But it's what she's done with her celebrity that really speaks to how she's impacted the city, the hospitality industry, and society at large. She's on the board of directors for Women Chefs and Restaurateurs as well as Boston Alliance of Lesbian Gay Bisexual Transgender Youth. She pushes the needle in the way it should be pushed. She's willing to talk about issues in her industry, such as wage disparity, sexual harassment, and diversity and inclusivity in workspaces. She always giving back, whether it's doing a cooking demonstration at Camp Harborview, taking part in a Big Sisters Association of Boston fashion show, or meeting with patients at Tufts Medical Center's floating hospital for children, Chef Faison is always looking for ways to make things better.

No matter how famous Tiffani has become, she's someone we can tell is appreciative to be in the restaurant business and who has never taken her position for granted. She's one of our favorite guests, but we know she'll have to check her TV schedule first, but that's to be expected. When you're a dynamo, everybody wants to watch.

BUTTERMILK FRIED CHICKEN SANDWICH WITH SMOKED JALAPEÑO GOO

Serves 6

This juicy chicken sandwich packs a spicy, slow burn—a lunch for the bold and the hungry.

To make the BBQ spice rub

1. Whisk everything together in a bowl, making sure to get out any lumps.

To prepare the chicken

1. In a mixing bowl, combine 1½ cups flour with 2 tablespoons BBQ spice rub.

2. Sprinkle this mixture on the chicken thighs and place them on a baking tray with a wire rack. Let this sit in the refrigerator, uncovered, for 1 to 3 hours (this is a good time to make your goo).

To make the jalapeño goo

1. While your chicken thighs are resting in the fridge, make your goo. Begin by roasting jalapeño peppers over a flame until charred or in a 400°F oven.

2. Heat olive oil on medium heat in a sauté pan and cook the onions for 5 to 10 minutes until soft.

3. Add the garlic and jalapeños, cook for another 2 minutes, seasoning with salt.

4. Transfer this mixture to a blender, adding the cream cheese and mayo. Blend until very smooth.

5. Transfer to a small bowl and refrigerate until ready to assemble.

To continue the chicken

1. In one bowl, combine the buttermilk, pickle juice, and egg with 2 tablespoons BBQ spice rub. Whisk until smooth. Put to the side until ready to fry.

2. In another bowl, combine the remaining 1½ cups flour, cornstarch, and the final 2 tablespoons BBQ spice rub.

3. When ready to fry, preheat a 5- to 6-quart stockpot halfway filled with canola oil to 325°F.

(Continued)

For the BBQ spice rub

- 3/4 cup kosher salt
- 1/8 cup white sugar
- 1/4 cup light brown sugar
- 1 teaspoon mustard powder
- 1 teaspoon smoked pimentón (paprika)
- 1 teaspoon fresh ground black pepper
- 1 teaspoon cayenne
- 1 teaspoon chili powder
- 1 teaspoon chipotle powder
- 2 teaspoons granulated onion
- 2 teaspoons granulated garlic

For the chicken

- 3 cups all-purpose flour, divided
- 6 boneless, skinless chicken thighs, pounded to an even thickness (about 1/2-inch thick)
- 2 cups buttermilk
- 1 cup pickle chips and their juice
- 1 egg
- 1 cup cornstarch
- 3–4 quarts canola oil for frying

For the sandwiches

- 6 seeded brioche or potato rolls, sliced in half
- 4 tablespoons unsalted butter

4. Place chicken into buttermilk mixture and let sit for 5 minutes.

5. Remove from buttermilk and place in flour/cornstarch mixture, gently pressing into the flour. Pat off any excess flour before gently lowering into the oil. Fry 3 thighs at a time for the best crunch.

6. When the internal temperature of the chicken reaches 165°F to 170°F, remove from oil and let drain on baking tray with rack. Season with salt as desired.

To make the sandwiches

1. While chicken is frying, griddle your rolls in the butter until golden brown.

2. Spread each side of the rolls with the jalapeño goo.

3. When chicken is ready, assemble sandwiches with pickles and enjoy!

For the jalapeño goo

- 3–4 jalapeños, seeded and peeled
- 2 tablespoons olive oil
- 1 cup minced white or Spanish onion
- 2 tablespoons minced garlic
- Kosher salt, to taste
- 8 ounces cream cheese, softened
- 1 cup mayonnaise, preferably Dukes

CHEF'S TIP: If you like your spice rub hotter, you can double, or even triple the cayenne.

Side Dish

CAMP HARBOR VIEW

Every kid deserves to have fun and formative summer camp experiences, and that's what the staff at Camp Harbor View has made happen for Boston's youth every year since 2007. This wonderful organization, which Jenny has been an advisory chair member of for ten years, began with a conversation between the late Mayor Tom Menino and one of the most prominent businessmen in the city, the late Jack Connors Jr.

They wanted to create a place where Boston's schoolchildren could play, learn, and have fun during the summer months. With Jack's vision, they found the perfect spot for the camp on Long Island in Boston Harbor.

Camp Harbor View has been a calling for Jack Connors. His ability to unify and his mentorship to those in the city, including us, has been immeasurable. He and his staff go beyond providing a safe, fun, and free space for kids in the summer. They also partner with youth and their families throughout the year with their Family Flex Fund, Leadership Academy, and their food access program among others.

Photo Courtesy of Camp Harbor View

Many of the campers had never seen the water until coming to Camp Harbor View, and the mission is to make sure the city is a place where every child can find joy as well as equity. Campers have summers they'll never forget, and it's been incredible to watch former campers grow into leaders who help shape the city. We've been proud to host their gala every year, and many of the chefs in this book have a special place for Camp Harbor View in their hearts, just like we do.

A Taste of Boston

KEN ORINGER

We like to playfully remind Chef Oringer from time to time that to us he's the restaurant community's Bradley Cooper. He's talented, charismatic, and he's the only person we've ever met who made *People* magazine's Hottest Bachelors list among the likes of George Clooney and Ben Affleck in 2002.

A lot has changed since then. All three bachelors are married, including Ken to his fabulous wife, Celine, but a part of us can't help ribbing the internationally renowned, contemplative, and generous James Beard Award–winning chef/restaurateur whenever we see him at one of his many successful restaurants. Uni, Toro, Coppa, Little Donkey, and Faccia a Faccia are on all the "best of" lists and where people go when they come to Boston. It's not the restaurants that are the tourist attractions, though; it's Chef Oringer and his gifts in the kitchen.

Born and bred in New Jersey, Chef Oringer's journey to culinary stardom began when he was a kid watching Julia Child on TV and enjoying trips to New York City restaurants with his family. After studying restaurant management at Bryant College in Rhode Island and earning a degree from The Culinary Institute of America, he began honing his chef skills across the country.

When Chef Oringer returned to Boston in 1997 and opened Clio in the Eliot Hotel, it marked a new wave of chef/owners who were expanding the Boston culinary scene and getting huge notice from the tastemakers of the nation.

Clio put Chef Oringer's vision under a spotlight when he was nominated for the James Beard Award four years in a row before winning Best Chef Northeast in 2001. He was getting national acclaim, appearing in magazines like *People* and on countless TV shows, including *Iron Chef America*. But since Clio, his vision has grown exponentially.

Being at Uni, which took over Clio at the Eliot Hotel, is like being in a Tokyo hotspot that offers exquisite sashimi and Asian street food right on Comm Ave. Toro, his Spanish tapas restaurant in the South End, is a constant party where guests are shoulder to shoulder with one another, unable to get enough of patatas bravas and empanadas—and the most delicious street corn!

If you're looking for incredible Italian, Chef Oringer has you covered with out-of-this-world pizza and small plates at Coppa in the South End, and coastal Italian fare at Faccia a Faccia on Newbury Street. And if you want a little bit of everything from pupusas to an unbelievable fried chicken sandwich, visit Little Donkey in Cambridge. And don't forget to order straight-up cookie dough for dessert.

Ken and Celine have two awesome kids. Their son Luca and their daughter Verveine, the namesake for Chef Oringer's bakery and café in Cambridge. Verveine has even co-authored a gluten-free cookbook with her dad aptly titled *Cooking with My Dad, the Chef*. We were so pleased to have the Chefs Oringers on our show making gluten-free spinach orecchiette together, and we loved seeing Ken look on with pride as his daughter helped prepare the dish. Cooking definitely runs in the family.

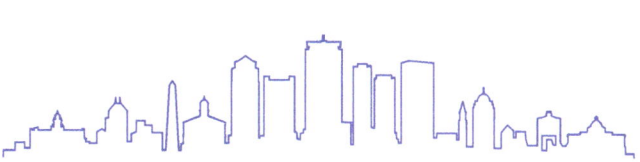

COPPA'S NDUJA PIZZA

Makes 1 pizza

Ndjua, a Calabrian sausage spread, will spice up your pizza and your palate in no time.

To make the sauce

1. Puree all ingredients together with a food processor or immersion blender. This can be stored in the refrigerator for 2 weeks or frozen for longer.

To make the pizza

1. Coat a smooth surface with flour to stretch the dough. The flour helps prevent the dough from sticking. If the dough still sticks, use a bit more flour.

2. When dough is nice and thin (9 to 10 inches around and 1/4 inch thick), place on a pizza stone.

3. Add a layer of sauce (about 1/2 cup) and cover with the mozzarella.

4. Distribute sausage around the pizza evenly.

5. Cook the pizza in a 500°F oven for 12 to 15 minutes, until crispy and golden brown. Remove from the oven and allow to cool for a minute.

6. Garnish with dollops of burrata, oregano leaves, chili flakes, and grated parmesan.

For the sauce

- 1 32-ounce can peeled, crushed tomatoes
- 2 garlic cloves
- 1/2 cup fresh basil
- 1 tablespoon sugar
- 1 teaspoon salt

For the pizza

- 1 8-ounce pizza dough (homemade or your favorite)
- Flour to stretch the dough
- 1/2 cup low-moisture mozzarella, shredded
- 1 ounce nduja sausage, crumbled
- 1 ounce fresh burrata, chopped
- Fresh oregano
- Chili flakes
- Grated parmesan to garnish

CHEF'S TIP: Go easy on the chili flakes on your pie if the nduja is too hot! There are enough leftover ingredients to make a second pizza.

A Taste of Boston

CARL DOOLEY

One of the things we're most proud of in the Boston culinary scene is how kind and generous people can be to each other. There's a camaraderie among chefs and kitchen staff across this city. We've seen that camaraderie at food galas where chefs were in competition for awards, and no matter who won, everyone celebrated one another. We've also seen it in the way chefs and restaurateurs promote each other's restaurants.

This special bond is especially true for kitchens that have mentor and mentee bonds. First, it's the teachers boosting the students. Then it can be the other way around. A lovely example of this kind of talent supporting talent is Carl Dooley, head chef at Mooncusser Fish House and its offshoot, Moon Bar.

Dooley worked under James Beard Award–winning chefs such as Eric Ripert and Frank Ruta. We met him when he was chef de cuisine at Craigie on Main, second in command to Tony Maws.

Maws's Craigie on Main was rustic and refined gourmet cuisine. The menu was constantly changing based on the best that local farms and local fishers had to offer. Nothing came pre-packaged, butchery was done in-house, every ingredient was treated with care, and everyone in the kitchen worked long hours and did everything with precision. Chef Dooley has said when he first started as a line cook, it was the hardest job he ever had. But he kept at it, worked at other restaurants in between, and eventually came back to Craigie on Main to become a collaborator with Chef Maws. This collaboration, and attention from guests and food critics, built Chef Dooley's confidence to know he could work anywhere and hold his own.

You may have seen Chef Dooley hold his own during his time as a competitor on season thirteen of *Top Chef*. His buoyant energy, his ability to elevate simple and fresh ingredients with bold spices, and the way he juggles many tasks but never shies away from hard work served him well on the show. It also serves him well at Mooncusser Fish House and Moon Bar.

He's re-energized the Back Bay seafood restaurant by creating a seasonally changing, multi-course, prix fixe menu that showcases local ingredients while giving them international flair. There are things he does with lamb, halibut, crab, or whatever comes his way that are nuanced, atypical, and mouthwatering. In a more casual mood? Visit Moon Bar across the street where the small plates include Mahi Mahi Ceviche, Tandoori Chicken Thighs with Cucumber Raita, and the Lamb Burger with Pickled Cauliflower and Tomato Chutney.

When we caught up with Chef Dooley, he was delighted to talk about his wife and two young kids and the work he was doing, but he also had a lot of wonderful things to say about his mentor, Tony.

He's still grateful for his mentor, and, we're sure, vice versa.

LAMB BURGER WITH PICKLED CAULIFLOWER AND TOMATO CHUTNEY

Serves 1

Tender, juicy, and perfect for the backyard grill, Chef Dooley's lamb burger is sure to delight the staunchest of hamburger devotees.

To make the tomato chutney

1. Bring a large pot of water to boil. Put the tomatoes in the boiling water for 1 to 2 minutes. You don't want the skin to blister. With a slotted spoon, transfer to a bowl. Let cool down enough to handle.

2. Once cool enough, peel the tomatoes, cut in half, and scoop the seeds out.

3. Roughly cut the tomatoes, transfer them to a pot, and bring to a boil. Reduce the heat to medium low and simmer for 10 minutes.

4. Let tomatoes cool down and then puree in a blender, food processor, or immersion blender. Set aside.

5. On medium-high heat, cook the garlic, ginger, onion, and chili in 1/4 cup canola oil until lightly caramelized, 5 to 8 minutes.

6. Add salt and pureed tomatoes, bring to a boil, simmer for 15 minutes until mixture thickens a bit. Blend this mixture in a food processor until smoothish.

7. Heat the remaining 1/4 cup canola oil with spices and curry leaf until they start to pop. Remove from heat and carefully add the pureed tomato mix.

8. Return to the stove and bring to a boil. Reduce heat and simmer for 10 minutes. Adjust with a bit of salt if needed.

9. Cool down and transfer to a jar or bowl until ready to serve. This can be sealed and stored in the refrigerator for up to 2 weeks.

To make the cauliflower pickles

1. Bring all the ingredients except the cauliflower to a boil.

2. Pour over the cauliflower and allow to cool to room temperature. These can be stored in a sealed container in the refrigerator for a few months.

(Continued)

For the tomato chutney

- 6 ripe beefsteak tomatoes
- 1/4 cup thinly sliced garlic
- 1/4 cup thinly sliced, peeled ginger
- 1/4 cup thinly sliced onion
- 1 fresno chili, cut in half, seeded, and thinly sliced
- 1/2 cup canola oil, divided
- 1 tablespoon salt
- 2 tablespoons black mustard seeds
- 1 tablespoon cumin seeds
- 1 tablespoon red chili flakes
- 1 teaspoon turmeric powder
- 12 curry leaves

For the pickled cauliflower

- 1 head of cauliflower
- 2 cups water
- 1 cup rice wine vinegar
- 1 teaspoon ground turmeric
- 1 tablespoon ground coriander seeds
- 1 tablespoon ground Kashmiri chili
- 1 tablespoon sugar
- 2 tablespoon salt

To make the burger

1. Grill or pan fry the burger to your liking, adding the cheese in the last minute of cooking.

2. Transfer to the onion roll and serve with the tomato chutney and pickled cauliflower.

For each burger

1 6-ounce ground lamb patty

1 slice cheddar cheese (Vermont Cabot is Chef Dooley's fav)

Onion roll, cut in half

> **Jenny:** When making this lamb burger, respect and honor the ingredients as Chef Dooley would.
>
> **Billy:** And have napkins at the ready after you enjoy every bite!

JATINDER SINGH AND SUPREET KAUR

Jenny here. Indian food has become a big part of my life since I started learning about Ayurveda, a holistic approach to mind and body health from India and Nepal. I have learned so much about the health benefits of spices and herbs in Indian cuisine and tried *many* different Indian restaurants. Bar none, and unequivocally without a shadow of a doubt, Mela on Tremont Street in the South End is the best Indian restaurant in the area, and father-daughter duo Jatinder Singh and Supreet Kaur have created a really special and authentic restaurant.

There's a tendency for restaurants to Americanize their cuisine, but since it came on the scene seventeen years ago, Mela has always stayed true to its flavor roots while modernizing classic dishes. *Mela* is a Sanskrit word that roughly translates to "gathering" or "festival," a place where people come together to celebrate and enjoy amazing food, and the name certainly fits this restaurant! There are mouth-watering staples like lamb biryani, samosas, and pakoras, but also new spins on old favorites like Duck Masala or Subz Panchmael, a stir-fried vegetable dish featuring artichokes; red, yellow, and green peppers; and asparagus in a tomato cardamom sauce.

A Taste of Boston

When my husband Rob and I lived in the South End, we were at Mela twice a week. We became regulars and sat at the same table inside the charming and warm dining room for years. Every time we visited, the hospitality from Jatinder and his staff was incredible, as was the service, but they only knew us as regulars and had no idea what I did for work. We were just a couple who really couldn't get enough of their veggie korma.

As years passed and our family grew, I became a new mom. My daughter, whom I was breastfeeding, was pretty sick at the time, and there were only certain things she could tolerate, which meant there were only certain things I could eat. I called Jatinder at Mela, explained to him that my daughter was sick, and asked him if it was possible for his chefs to cook a few dishes for us using ghee instead of oil? He said, "Of course, just call me in the morning when you're ready to order so I can give the chefs enough time to prepare." It's always that kindness that I will remember, and it's the same kind of warm and above and beyond hospitality they show to each guest.

Now that my daughters are older and their palates have expanded, we've been able to go to Mela as a family and introduce them to new foods, which is awesome. Though we don't live as close as we did, Mela will always be our go-to for veggie korma!

SHAHI NAVRATAN KORMA

Serves 4 to 6

This "nine-gem" korma is fit for a king and queen—a royal treat for cold winter nights or rainy afternoons.

1. Heat ghee in a skillet over medium heat. Add onions; cook and stir until tender and translucent, 2 to 3 minutes. Stir in garlic and ginger; cook and stir until fragrant, about 1 minute.

2. Stir in carrots, potatoes, zucchini, yellow squash, cauliflower, tomato sauce, cashews, red and green peppers, and chili pepper. Season with curry powder and salt; cook and stir until potatoes are tender, about 10 minutes.

3. Stir in cream or coconut milk and the peas, reduce heat to low, cover, and simmer for 15 to 20 minutes until the vegetables are soft and still intact and the peas are cooked. Garnish with cilantro and serve with basmati rice or naan bread.

- 1½ tablespoons ghee
- 1 small onion, diced
- 4 cloves garlic, minced
- 1 teaspoon minced fresh ginger root
- 4 carrots, cubed
- 2 potatoes, cubed
- 1/2 zucchini, cubed
- 1/2 yellow squash, cubed
- 1/2 cauliflower, chopped
- 1 (6-ounce) can tomato sauce
- 3 tablespoons ground, unsalted cashews
- 1/2 green bell pepper, chopped
- 1/2 red bell pepper, chopped
- 1 fresh green chili pepper, finely chopped
- 2 tablespoons curry powder
- 2½ teaspoons salt
- 2 cups heavy cream or coconut milk
- 1 cup frozen green peas
- 1 bunch fresh cilantro for garnish

ANDY HUSBANDS

We have so much respect and admiration for chef and restaurateur Andy Husbands. Not only because he's brought exceptional barbeque to Boston with his six Smoke Shop BBQ locations, but because he's genuine, says what needs to be said when advocating for the hospitality industry, and is so passionate about teaching others what barbecue means to him and how it can best bring people together. The author of six successful cookbooks and the champion of many Jack Daniel's World Championship Invitational Barbecue competitions with his IQUE BBQ team, Chef Husbands teaches classes at his restaurants for people who want to learn from the Professor of the Pit himself.

When we've seen him teach a class or work in the kitchen, he'll take a giant chunk of brisket, walk someone step by step on how much fat should be trimmed and why, show how he makes a rub with different spices and why each spice is so crucial, and tells the stories of the origins of the meat and the culture of barbecue so that the whole process matters to you. We've realized he does all of this not because it's his job, but because this is his dream.

The dream began after graduating from Johnson & Wales and working at some local kitchens, including East Coast Grill, where Chef Husbands was mentored by Chris Schlesinger. He then opened Tremont 647 with his best friend from Needham High, Chris Hart. It was an American restaurant with global influences—and an incredible pajama brunch that featured a breakfast pizza with a fried egg on top. But it turned out that barbeque was more his thing. After decades of being on the competitive barbecue circuit with the IQUE BBQ team, Chef Husbands decided to bring his love and passion for "city Q"—barbeque that doesn't necessarily have to come from places in the South and Midwest known for BBQ—to Boston. With Smoke Shop BBQ locations in Harvard and Kendall Squares in Cambridge, Assembly Row in Somerville, East Boston, the Seaport, and Hub Hall in TD Garden, Chef Husbands and his crew let it be known that it doesn't matter where the barbeque comes from, it just has to be the best barbeque you've ever tasted.

We highly recommend giving The PitMaster from Husband's menu a try with a friend or two. It features a sampler of *all* the Smoke Shop's meats and sides, including the tender Texas-style brisket, the delicate pulled pork, smoked turkey breast, BBQ chicken, pimento mac and cheese, zucchini salad, Vidalia onion mashed potatoes, and a whole lot more. If you have any room left, go for the Gooey Butter Cake, a decadent pound cake with a cream cheese topping that will have you smiling right before you nod off for a nap.

When Chef Husbands isn't smoking meats and running his BBQ empire, he's hanging with his lovely wife and twin daughters, serving as vice president at the Massachusetts Restaurant Association, appearing on TV shows like the Cooking Channel's *Burgers, Brew & 'Que*, and raising awareness for organizations like Rosie's Place and Share Our Strength.

He even managed to find time to teach us how to make the Smoke Shop's famous chicken wings and set up a contest for us on our show. It was stiff competition, but Jenny ended up making the better wing. Sorry, Billy.

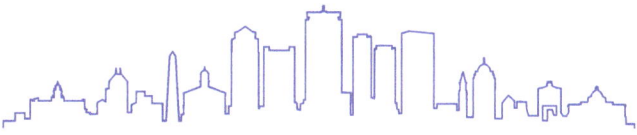

PORK BELLY BANH MI

Serves: 10 to 12

This Vietnamese sandwich with American barbecue fillings is a work of art made better by the process of smoking the meat. The rub can be put together in a few minutes with items from the pantry and tastes great on chicken too! If you're looking for a little more spice, use serrano peppers instead of jalapeño.

To make the pork barbecue rub

1. Combine all the ingredients in a bowl and mix thoroughly. This can be stored in a cool, dark place in an airtight container for up to several months.

To make the Smoky Hot BBQ Sauce

1. Combine the molasses, vinegar, and brown and granulated sugars in a medium saucepan over medium-high heat and bring to a boil, stirring occasionally.

2. Add jalapeños, Worcestershire sauce, tomato paste, garlic powder, hickory powder, cumin, mustard, thyme, and anise or fennel seeds. Stir well to incorporate.

3. Reduce heat and simmer for 5 minutes, stirring occasionally.

4. Whisk in ketchup and salt and simmer for 2 minutes more.

5. Cool to room temperature and refrigerate in an airtight container for up to 1 month.

To make the Pork Belly Burnt Ends

1. Combine the water, brown sugar, salt, fish sauce, cumin seeds, fennel seeds, garlic, and red pepper flakes in a large pot over high heat and bring to a boil. Stir occasionally until the sugar and salt have dissolved.

2. Remove from the heat, cool and refrigerate overnight.

3. Place the pork belly in the chilled brine, cover, and refrigerate for 3 days, flipping every day.

4. Preheat smoker to 275°F about 30 minutes before you are ready to cook. Stoke the fire with hardwood; we prefer cherry wood for this.

5. Remove pork belly from the brine and pat dry. Lightly dust the pork all over with 1 cup of the prepared barbecue rub and insert the

For the pork barbecue rub

- 4 tablespoons paprika
- 2 tablespoons packed light brown sugar
- 2 tablespoons kosher salt
- 2 tablespoons chili powder
- 2 tablespoons ground cumin
- 3 tablespoons coarsely ground black pepper
- 1 tablespoon cayenne pepper

For the Smoky Hot BBQ Sauce

- 1/2 cup blackstrap molasses
- 1/2 cup apple cider vinegar
- 1/2 cup packed dark brown sugar
- 1/2 cup granulated sugar
- 1 cup thinly sliced jalapeño peppers (3 to 4 large jalapeños)
- 2 tablespoons Worcestershire sauce
- 1 tablespoon tomato paste
- 1 teaspoon garlic powder
- 1 teaspoon hickory powder
- 1 teaspoon cumin seeds, toasted and ground
- 1 teaspoon yellow mustard seeds
- 1/2 teaspoon dried thyme
- 1/2 anise or fennel seeds
- 2 cups ketchup
- 2 teaspoons kosher salt

thermometer probe into the side of the meat. Smoke for 2 to 3 hours to an internal temperature of 180°F.

6. Remove from the smoker and allow to rest on a cutting board for 10 minutes. Cut into 1-inch cubes. Place the cubes on a wire rack and put the rack in the smoker for 1 hour more.

7. Meanwhile, in a small saucepan over medium heat, warm the barbecue sauce.

8. When pork belly cubes are done, remove from the smoker and toss in a large bowl with the warmed barbecue sauce and remaining 1/4 cup barbecue rub. Toss to coat evenly.

9. Spread the cubes on a baking sheet and return to the smoker for 45 minutes to 1¼ hours, until the sauce is caramelized and sticky to the touch.

10. Remove from the smoker and cool for 15 minutes before serving. If you're not ready to serve these, they can be refrigerated in a tightly sealed container for up to 5 days.

To make the banh mi

1. Toss carrots, cucumber, daikon, radishes, red onion, jalapeño, and garlic in a large mixing bowl until incorporated.

2. Mix in the sugar and salt and let sit for 5 minutes. Add the vinegar, lime juice, and fish sauce and let the vegetables sit for at least 10 minutes more. Drain.

3. In a medium bowl, mix together the mayonnaise and sriracha.

To finish

1. To assemble the banh mi, slice each roll horizontally halfway through and spread open like a book.

2. Spread about 2 tablespoons liver mousse on the bottom half of the roll, if using, and spread about 1 tablespoon sriracha mayonnaise on the top half.

3. Pile about 3/4 cup pork belly over the mousse and top with 1/3 to 1/2 cup vegetables. Garnish with the mint and cilantro.

CHEF'S TIP: The pickled vegetables can be refrigerated in a tightly sealed container for up to three days. The Sriracha Mayo can be refrigerated in a tightly sealed container for up to five days.

For the Pork Belly Burnt Ends

1 gallon water

1/2 cup packed light brown sugar

1/2 cup kosher salt

2 tablespoons fish sauce

1 tablespoon cumin seeds, toasted

1 teaspoon fennel seeds

8 cloves garlic, smashed

2 teaspoons red pepper flakes

5 pounds pork belly, skin off

For the banh mi

4 medium carrots, coarsely shredded (about 3 cups)

1/2 English cucumber, sliced (about 2 cups)

1/4 diakon, sliced thin

8 radishes, thinly sliced (about 1/2 cup)

1/4 cup julienned red onion

1 small jalapeño pepper, seeded and thinly sliced into rings (about 1/3 cup)

3 cloves garlic

3 tablespoons sugar

1 tablespoon kosher salt

1/4 cup rice wine vinegar

Juice of 1 lime

2 tablespoons fish sauce

1 cup mayonnaise

2 tablespoons sriracha

For the finish

10–12 6-inch baguettes or sub rolls

1¼ cups liver mousse

1 bunch fresh mint sprigs

1 bunch fresh cilantro sprigs

PAUL WAHLBERG

We couldn't write a book about where to eat in Boston without bringing up one of the city's biggest success stories from one of our favorite families. You may have heard of them. We were at the opening of the first Wahlburgers in the Hingham Shipyard back in 2011, and since then the restaurant empire has grown to a hundred locations all over the country, Canada, and even in Australia and New Zealand.

The Wahlbergs are no strangers to worldwide recognition. Donnie is in one of the biggest bands in the world and acts on the show *Blue Bloods,* and Mark is an A-list actor, producer, and entrepreneur. But it's the food at Wahlburgers, and their sister restaurant Alma Nove in Hingham, that are the stars we can't get enough of, and Chef Paul Wahlberg is the star maker.

Chef Wahlberg grew up one of nine kids in a loving and boisterous Dorchester family. He says he didn't have much of a singing voice or the passion for acting, but he did fall in love with food at the age of twelve when he bit into an eggplant parmesan sandwich at his friend's house. From then on, his culinary passions took flight. He cooked in the kitchen with his wonderful mother Alma for family dinners, and as a teenager, he washed dishes at his friend's family restaurant and worked as a caterer.

After graduating high school, he worked at many local restaurant kitchens, including the ones at The Charles Hotel and The Four Seasons, and eventually became executive chef at Bridgeman's in Hull, captaining that kitchen for nine years. But he always thought about the family dinners he had in his childhood, the food that brought his loved ones together. He wanted to bring that good feeling to the people in his neighborhood. And so, Wahlburgers—an ode to Chef Wahlberg's upbringing, the food he loved, and the people in his life for whom he's always cooking—was born.

With Boston locations in Fenway and at Logan airport, Wahlburgers doesn't only serve burgers. The menus feature items such as Crispy Fried Pickles, Parmesan Truffle Tots, Salmon and Street Corn Salad, and the Crispy Fish Sandwich.

Donnie's favorite is the BBQ Bacon Burger topped with white cheddar, bacon, fresh jalapeños, BBQ sauce, and avocado spread. Mark's favorite is The Impossible Burger, a plant-based burger topped with smoked cheddar, lettuce, caramelized onions, housemade chili-spiced tomatoes, and Wahl Sauce. But it's Chef Wahlberg's favorite—the Our Burger with lettuce, tomato, government cheese, onion, pickles, and signature Wahl Sauce—that speaks to how keeping things simple is sometimes the best.

We've been fortunate to be in the Wahlberg family's orbit for many years, promoting and supporting their endeavors and seeing how much they give back to their communities, locally and globally. Their reality show *Wahlburgers* gave people a taste of their culinary story. But the reality of how generous Chef Wahlberg is in giving his time and resources to the South Shore and North Shore YMCA, The Boys and Girls Club, and Mass Eye and Ear, among others, is well known to us when we work with him at galas and events championing these organizations.

Even after many years of friendship, we still don't know what is in the Wahl Sauce. But knowing Chef Wahlberg, we're pretty sure one of the ingredients is love of family. He's got one of the best.

SEARED SALMON WITH RHUBARB VINAIGRETTE, BLACK RICE, AND MINTED CUCUMBER

Serves 4

This recipe makes a meal that's meant to be shared with family. It's the Wahlberg way. It's a good idea to prepare the rhubarb vinaigrette the day before and store it in the refrigerator.

To make the rhubarb vinaigrette

1. In a small, non-reactive saucepan add the rhubarb, water, bay leaf, vinegar, sugar, shallot, and grenadine (or raspberries), and simmer for 5 to 8 minutes until bubbly and rhubarb softens.

2. Set aside to cool for 5 minutes, then remove bay leaf and place in a blender.

3. Puree on low, add the thyme, and slowly stream in the olive oil.

4. Season with salt and pepper and taste.

5. Transfer to an 8-ounce plastic squeeze bottle and store in the refrigerator until the following day.

To make the minted cucumber

1. Mix all ingredients, taste for seasoning, and reserve.

To start the black rice

1. Rinsed rice under cold water in a fine mesh strainer.

2. In medium-size pot, add rice and 3 quarts cold water, bay leaf, salt, and onion.

3. Bring to a boil and then reduce to a simmer.

4. Simmer until tender, 45 to 60 minutes.

5. Strain and spread out on a sided cookie tray until cooled, then transfer to a storage container. This can be done same day or a day ahead and stored in the refrigerator.

To make the seared salmon

1. Pat your salmon filets dry with a paper towel and season with salt and pepper.

2. Let rest for 3 to 4 minutes.

For the rhubarb vinaigrette

- 2 stalks fresh rhubarb, peeled and sliced into 1-inch thick slices
- 1/4 cup water
- 1 bay leaf
- 1 tablespoon good quality red wine vinegar
- 1 tablespoon sugar
- 1 small shallot, thinly sliced
- 1 tablespoon grenadine, or 6 frozen raspberries (for color)
- 1/2 teaspoon chopped fresh thyme
- 1/2 cup olive oil
- Salt and pepper, to taste

For the minted cucumber

- 1/2 cup peeled, seeded, and fine-diced English cucumber
- 1/2 teaspoon chopped mint leaves
- 1/2 teaspoon chopped fresh parley
- 1 teaspoon extra-virgin olive oil

3. Heat a large nonstick or well-seasoned cast iron skillet over medium high heat and add the oil, let sit for a minute, and then heat for 1 minute (oil should begin to smoke a bit).

4. Carefully place the salmon, skin side down, in the skillet (make sure you leave space between the filets).

5. Turn the heat on high and cook for 3 to 4 minutes, you will see the skin edges turn golden brown.

6. Sprinkle with the chopped thyme and flip the salmon with a slotted spatula.

7. Place the skillet in the oven and cook for 5 minutes.

8. Remove the pan from the oven and transfer the salmon to a platter to rest for 3 to 4 minutes.

To finish the black rice

1. While the salmon is cooking, melt the butter and mix in the prepared rice.

2. Add the stock and parsley. Warm for 3 to 4 minutes, seasoning with salt and pepper as needed.

To pull it all together

1. Stripe a plate with the rhubarb vinaigrette.

2. Place a mound of rice in the center of the plate.

3. Place salmon on a slight angle off of the rice and top the salmon with a tablespoon of the minted cucumber.

- 1 small radish, washed and finely diced
- 1/4 teaspoon fresh lemon juice
- Salt and pepper, to taste

For the black rice (to start)

- 1/2 pound black rice (can be purchased at a fine quality Italian grocery store or online)
- 1 bay leaf
- 1 teaspoon salt
- 1 cup diced onion

For the seared salmon

- 4 6-ounce fresh salmon filets, scaled (good quality farm-raised works perfectly, or wild caught)
- 1/2 teaspoons salt
- 1/2 teaspoon pepper
- 1 tablespoon olive or canola oil
- 1/2 teaspoon chopped fresh thyme

For the black rice (to finish)

- 1/2 cup chicken or vegetable stock
- 2 tablespoons butter
- Salt and pepper, to taste
- 1/3 cup chopped fresh Italian parsley

JOE MILANO AND AMERICO DIFRONZO

Pictured: Chef Americo DiFronzo

There are tourist spots that if you've lived here your whole life, you may never visit in order to avoid the out-of-town crowds. We love to remind local people that they're allowed to go to Union Oyster House—and they should.

The iconic spot is a destination for tourists from all over the world who walk down cobblestone streets near Faneuil Hall, looking to learn everything about American history. And the restaurant gives them plenty.

If you'd like to sit where JFK sat, Proprietor Joe Milano can show you to the Kennedy Booth. If you'd like to lean like Daniel Webster at the soapstone oyster bar while watching shuckers get oysters ready, or learn about the oldest newspaper in the country, the *Massachusetts Spy*, which was printed there in 1771 before the building was a restaurant, Joe can tell you all about it.

Bostonians shouldn't forget—this place is for you too. Joe makes sure that beyond preserved history, there's a fantastic menu. And the talent behind that menu is Executive Chef Americo DiFronzo (pictured here). Chef DiFronzo serves the kind of chowder and oysters that will have a native Bay Stater nodding with approval.

Trained in classical cuisine, Chef DiFronzo has thirty-eight years of experience under his belt, as he has worked for many restaurants in the greater Boston area. He has so many accolades and is a part of so many culinary organizations that it would take a whole book to mention them all!

He's one of only eight hundred fellows of the American Academy of Chefs, is the first chef from Massachusetts to be inducted into Les Disciples d'Escoffier International, USA, and is responsible for the Union Oyster House earning an Achievement of Excellence Award from the American Culinary Federation in 2014. He's also a culinary arts instructor at Boston University's School of Hospitality and Administration and Management, giving lessons to the next generation of executive chefs and restaurateurs.

Chef DiFronzo (photographed here) has been with the Union Oyster House for years, and he and his staff know how to prepare any kind of fare from the sea in the restaurant's modernized kitchen. We're partial to Chef DiFronzo's lobster roll in the summer, and he's graciously provided the recipe.

As much as the Union Oyster House is an institution for the city, so is owner Joe Milano.

He's the first person to lend a hand of support through press, promotion, donations, or his time and energy. He has welcomed countless people to Boston, whether it's a TV crew shooting a pilot like HBO's *Julia* in his restaurant or guests wanting to know more about the original chairs from Fenway Park that are on display. There have been only three families to own the Union Oyster House, and we hope the Milano family—which includes his lovely wife of forty-nine years Jill, his four daughters, and his nine grandchildren—keep it in their loving care for years to come.

NEW ENGLAND LOBSTER ROLL WITH FRENCH FRIES

Serves 4

Chef Rico DiFronzo makes the quintessential lobster roll. Tradition never tasted so good.

To make the lobster salad

1. In a large bowl, lightly mix lobster meat, celery, salt, pepper, lemon juice, and parsley.
2. Add mayonnaise and gently mix until mayonnaise is incorporated.

To make the French fries

1. Place oil in a heavy-bottom pan and heat to no higher than 325°F. When the oil is hot, add the fries slowly and cook for about 5 minutes. Remove and drain on a paper towel. This is a good time to add your favorite seasoning to the fries.

To finish

1. While the fries are cooking, butter the brioche rolls, then grill to a golden brown.
2. Once the bread is toasted, it is time to assemble your lobster rolls. Slice rolls end to end halfway down. Place one lettuce leaf in each roll and then add 5 ounces of lobster salad.
3. Serve with fries and a dill pickle.

For the lobster salad

1¼ pounds fresh cooked lobster meat (cut into 1-inch pieces)

3 tablespoons minced celery

1/4 teaspoon salt

1/8 teaspoon ground white pepper

1½ teaspoons fresh lemon juice

2 teaspoons finely chopped parsley

1/3 cup extra heavy mayonnaise

For the French fries

32 ounces canola oil

24 ounces French fries

For the finish

2 tablespoons butter

4 sub-shaped brioche rolls

4 leaves green leaf lettuce (washed and dried)

4 dill pickle spears

JOE FARO AND NIMESH MAHARJAN

Pictured: Chef Nimesh Maharjan

If you are a friend of Joe Faro's, you're his family. We're honored to have had a front-row seat as Joe has grown his Tuscan Brands empire to immense proportions.

We first met Joe at the start of Tuscan Brands at his Tuscan Kitchen restaurant in Salem, New Hampshire. Within five minutes of meeting him, we had the sense that this guy can do anything he wants. And he has.

His love of made-from-scratch Italian cuisine has produced authentic restaurants, retail, and hospitality experiences like Toscana Italian Chophouse & Wine Bar in Portsmouth, New Hampshire; two massive Tuscan Markets in Salem and Portsmouth, New Hampshire; Tuscan Sea Grill in Newburyport, Massachusetts; Artisan Chef Catering Company; and two more Tuscan Kitchens in Burlington, Massachusetts, and in the Seaport of Boston.

He also has a *whole Tuscan Village,* a mixed-use, 170-acre property in Salem, New Hampshire. At Joe's village, you can go to the Tuscan Market and buy Italian everything, from imported cheeses to olive oil to meats. Or maybe sitting in on a cooking demonstration to see how to make pizza and pasta at home from the Tuscan staff is more your style. You can also enjoy the beer garden, grab a lobster roll at the Beach Plum, shop at stores such as L.L. Bean and Pottery Barn, lounge by the Artisan Hotel's luxury pool, or even kayak in a manmade lake full of fish. And if you *really* love the Tuscan Village, you can live there in your very own luxury apartment.

And how did all this start? Joe grew up in Lawrence, Massachusetts, in a Sicilian family. His parents immigrated from Sicily, met in Lawrence, and raised a family while running their Italian American bakery in Haverhill. Joe learned all about hard work from his family's business, but knew that while he loved food, he wanted to do something big. We've found with Joe *everything* is big—his generosity, his energy, his love for his wife and kids, and his vision.

During Joe's senior year at the University of New Hampshire (Go Wildcats! Representing Jenny's alma mater) he had to write up a proposal for a hypothetical company. This college assignment turned into a real-life business proposal that set in motion Joseph's Gourmet Pasta and Sauces, a multi-million-dollar business that was bought by Nestle Prepared Foods. This deal set Joe up for retirement, but we can't imagine Joe *ever retiring*.

Tuscan Kitchen in the Seaport is an artisan Italian experience where bread, pasta, gelato, and desserts are made from scratch and the ambience of the 300-seat restaurant is rustic yet elegant.

Faro makes a lot of business decisions, but his best one? Hiring Executive Chef Nimesh Maharjan (photographed here), whose talent has been the ability to bring Joe's vision to life.

Chef Maharjan came to Nantucket from Katmandu, Nepal, in 2006 and learned much from Todd English while working at 29 Fair. Chef Maharjan has been with Joe and the Tuscan brand since 2016, and his leadership in the kitchen, focus on details, and passion for Italian cooking with local ingredients has made Tuscan Kitchen Seaport the dining destination for all things *delizioso*. There's nobody who can make *cacio e pepe* like he can!

Fun fact: When Jenny was on her honeymoon with her husband Rob in Nepal, in a country of millions of people, they were able to find Nimesh's brother and sing Chef Maharjan's praises together. It was a very special memory among many special memories with our friend Nimesh.

Speaking of memories, we've had a *ton* with both Joe and Nimesh. From Joe coming on to co-host our show, cooking demonstrations at Tuscan Village, and working together at events for non-profits. We can't wait to see what Joe and Tuscan Brands come up with next.

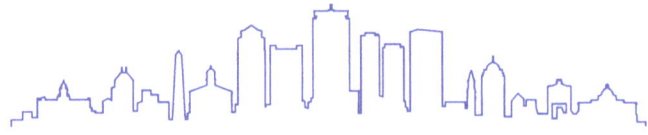

CACIO E PEPE

Serves 4

Cacio e pepe is a classic Roman pasta dish known for its simplicity and deliciousness. While traditionally made with long pasta like spaghetti, we adapted it for cappelini pasta.

1. Bring a large pot of salted water to a boil.
2. Cook the pasta according to package instruction for al dente, reserving 1/2 cup pasta cooking water before draining.
3. While pasta is cooking, mix the cheese and pepper in a bowl.
4. In a large pan, add the cooked and drained pasta.
5. Sprinkle half of the cheese and pepper mixture over the pasta and toss well.
6. Gradually add the reserved pasta cooking water, continuing to toss the pasta until it's well coated, and a creamy sauce forms. Adjust the amount of water as needed.
7. Add the remaining cheese and pepper mixture, tossing again to ensure even coating.
8. Stir in unsalted butter for an extra creamy finish if desired.
9. Serve immediately while the pasta is hot, grinding some additional black pepper on top if desired.

- 14 ounces cappelini pasta (Tuscan or your favorite brand)
- 1½ cups pecorino Romano cheese, finely grated
- 2 teaspoons coarsely ground black pepper, more for garnish if desired
- 2 tablespoons unsalted butter (optional)
- Salt, to taste

CHEF'S TIP: This dish is all about the simplicity of quality ingredients, so be sure to use a good quality pecorino Romano cheese for the best flavor.

BRENDAN PELLEY

Chef Brendan Pelley is a very patient person. We know this because we have tried to pronounce *many* Greek dishes and culinary terms over, and over, and over again in their presence. Occasionally we get some right, but most of the time, we never quite figure it out, and Chef Pelley does not judge us. The culinary director of Xenia Greek Hospitality Group, who oversees the operation of food concepts such as Bar Vlaha, Krasi, Greco, Agora, and Hecate, never tires of our many attempts during our visits.

The ancient Greek concept of *xenia* is roughly translated to making a guest or a stranger a friend through hospitality, gifts, food, and warmth. The Xenia Greek Hospitality Group, led by Demetri Tsolakis and Stefanos Ougrinis, is doing just that for guests at their restaurants.

There's the fast casual Greco with locations in Back Bay, the Seaport, Downtown, and Hub Hall; Agora market with products from Greece in the Seaport; sophisticated Krasi Meze and Wine Bar in Back Bay; hideaway cocktail bar Hecate in Back Bay; and Bar Vlaha in Brookline, which is like stepping into a *yiayia's* (grandmother) home for regional Vlach specialties. Who better to be in charge of these delicious Greek concepts than Chef Pelley, who has an outstanding resume, handled the flames of *Hell's Kitchen*, and is of Greek heritage on their father's side of the family?

Growing up in Chelmsford, Massachusetts, some of Chef Pelley's fondest culinary memories were the smells of roast lamb and spanakopita at their Papou's home for Sunday dinners. As a teenager, Chef Pelley worked as a busser and dishwasher at Friendly's before finding work at local Greek pizza shops. They worked their way up, helming kitchens as executive chef at Zebra Bistro in Medfield; Michael Schlow's Doretta Taverna & Raw Bar; their pop-up Pelekasis (the Pelley family's original last name), which was a Best of Boston winner in 2016; and Gibbet Hill Grill in Groton.

You may have seen Chef Pelley on season 14 of *Hell's Kitchen* or on *Beat Bobby Flay*, but we highly encourage you to visit Bar Vlaha in Brookline to behold Brendan's star power. Bar Vlaha showcases the regional cuisine of the Vlach people, nomadic shepherds who live in central and northern Greece. Chef Pelley and members of the Xenia Group traveled to Greece and the Vlaha region to research the food and techniques used in the mountainous villages, and their eye-opening travels helped create one of the most unique restaurants in the greater Boston area.

When you walk into Bar Vlaha, the aromas from the stone oven and open charcoal grill welcome you as you take in the vibrant photographs of the Vlach people on the walls. There are bright textiles and fabrics from the region adorning the furniture, and house-baked sourdough bread ready to be dipped in spreads such as *galotyri* (soft goat and sheep cheese). The seasonally changing menu speaks to Chef Pelley's dedication of using sustainable and local foods.

Whether you're at Bar Vlaha for dinner to feast on *Agriogourouno* (wild boar shoulder in red wine and spices served with soft cheese) or there for brunch to enjoy cocktails such as Pump the Briki, the menu will make you say, "Opa!" Now that's a word we have no trouble pronouncing, especially when dining on Chef Pelley's food.

SOURDOUGH BREAK BAR VLAHA STYLE

Makes 2 loaves

Crusty, magnificent sourdough made for dipping into mezze spreads and dips. Olive oil is also a great option. This is a multi-day-process recipe that requires some patience.

Day 1

1. Place 3 cups water in large mixing bowl. Add starter and mix.
2. Mix in sifted flours and allow to *autolyse* (hydrate) for 1 hour.
3. Add salt and remaining water and pinch into dough and let sit for 1/2 hour.
4. Bulk stretch and fold 5 times every 1/2 hour until dough passes windowpane test (stretch a bit of the dough to see if light comes through), then let it rise by 30 percent.
5. Divide dough in half and allow it to rest on a clean counter.
6. Divide and shape into balls. Evenly flour the tops, cover, and let rest 1/2 hour.
7. Gently flip each dough ball onto floured side and pull corners and sides to form seams and pinch.
8. Place dough balls, seam side up, into rice-flour-coated bannetons. Place in refrigerator to let cold ferment overnight.

Day 2

1. Preheat Dutch oven(s) in the oven at 500°F for 30 to 60 minutes, then drop oven temperature to 450°F.
2. Remove Dutch oven(s) and flip each dough ball out of banneton and into Dutch oven. Score the tops of dough, place lid on the Dutch oven, and return to oven for 20 minutes.
3. Remove Dutch oven lids and bake loaves for an additional 20 minutes.
4. Remove and let cool for 1 hour on wire rack before slicing.

- 3 cups water, plus 1/4 cup
- 7½ cups all-purpose unbleached flour, sifted (King Arthur brand preferred)
- 3/4 cup whole wheat flour, sifted
- 1 cup sourdough starter (leaven)
- 3 teaspoons kosher salt
- Rice flour for dusting

CHEF'S TIP: This delicious bread can be served with simple meze such as marinated kalamata olives (olive oil, slivered garlic, fresh thyme and oregano, orange zest) and sheep's milk feta cheese (drizzle with olive oil and dry Greek oregano rigani) or with brined hot peppers such as pepperoncini or marinated roasted red peppers.

COLTON COBURN-WOOD

Cósmica in The Revolution Hotel in the South End had just opened when the pandemic hit. We wanted to continue to highlight restaurants at a time when we were all stuck at home, so we would Zoom with chefs for our Home-Cooking Heroes segments. When Billy Zoomed in with Cósmica's executive chef Colton Coburn-Wood to show our viewers how to make nachos, Chef Coburn-Wood's playful nature, youthful energy, and wide smile were on full display even during a very stressful time. No matter what the circumstances, it's clear he's always going to be creating wonderfully funky dishes and having a lot of fun doing it.

Cósmica, sister restaurant to The Beehive, which is also owned by the Wildlife Hospitality Group, is serving traditional Mexican street food while using local New England ingredients and bringing Chef Coburn-Wood's own style to each dish. It hasn't always been easy to find excellent Mexican food in Boston, but oh how Cósmica has delivered.

With constantly changing dinner and late-night menus that feature incredible street tacos, enchiladas stuffed with ingredients you wouldn't expect such as mashed potatoes, and seafood such as cod being used in the mole de la casa, Cósmica is bolstering Mexican flavors in its own fun and unique way. Many of the dishes are or can be made gluten-free, and there are veggie-friendly plates like Cauliflower á la Cósmica (served with chipotle pineapple, salsa roja, and a pepita crumble), and vacation cocktails like the frozen Cósmica Painkiller, as well as a rotating margarita menu with new flavors featured all the time.

Chef Coburn-Wood grew up in Massachusetts, hanging out in the kitchen as his mother and grandmother cooked mostly French and Italian food. But it was during his time in California as a teenager where he grew to love Mexican and Mexi-Cali food. He came back to Boston, building up his resume by working at Hamersley's Bistro, Petit Robert Bistro, and at Ashmont Grill with Chef Chris Douglass, who became Colton's culinary mentor as well as father-in-law when Colton married Chef Douglass's daughter, Emma.

He's traveled to many parts of Mexico to learn more about the culture and craft, and he's found a home with the Wildlife Hospitality Group, trusted to be at the helm of Cósmica since its opening.

You can find Chef Coburn-Wood's latest inventive creations on his Instagram page, where he shares what's going on in the Cósmica kitchen and bites into secret tacos that only members of the Cósmica Secret Taco Society can order with a password. Trust us, you'll want the password. These are wild tacos.

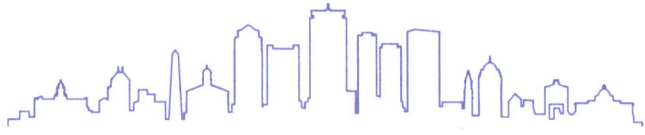

CONCHITA PIBIL TACOS

Serves 24

A slow-cooked Yucatan classic, these tacos are fun to assemble, full of flavor, and juicy. Make sure to have plenty of napkins at the ready.

To make the pibil marinade

1. Toast spices until fragrant and then place in a blender with all other ingredients and blend until smooth.

To make the pork

1. Place pork shoulder in a large baking dish.
2. Pour pibil marinade over the top, cover, and place in fridge overnight.
3. The next morning, season chilled pork shoulder with salt, and wrap in banana leaves (or foil).
4. Place in a roasting pan and cover tightly. Cook at 350°F for 3 hours or until pork pulls apart easily.
5. Pull pork and mix in cooking juices and leftover marinade to taste.

To make the guacamolio

1. Blend all ingredients in blender until smooth and set aside. **Note:** This must be made day of serving the tacos.

To make the pickled red onions

1. In a mixing bowl, mix sugar, salt, and white vinegar together. Pour over onions and submerge by using a plate to keep them in the liquid.

To finish

1. Heat tortillas in a pan a few seconds on each side, until they become soft and warm. Spoon quacamolio on tortilla, add a good helping of pork, garnish with pickled onions and cilantro.

For the pibil marinade

- 3/4 cup fresh oregano
- 3/4 cup achiote paste
- 1 teaspoon cloves
- 1 teaspoon allspice
- 4 cinnamon sticks
- 3 yellow onions
- 10 garlic cloves, peeled
- 4 tablespoons black peppercorns
- 6 bay leaves
- 1¼ cup white vinegar
- 4 cups canola oil
- 4 cups orange juice

For the pork

- 1 6-pound pork shoulder
- Salt to taste
- 1 pound banana leaves or foil

For the guacamolio

- 2 avocados
- 3 serrano chili peppers
- 1 Anaheim chili pepper, stemmed and seeded
- 1/2 bunch cilantro
- 1/4 cup lime juice
- Salt, to taste

For the pickled red onions

- 4 red onions, peeled, julienned
- 1/3 cup sugar
- 1/3 cup salt
- 4 cups white vinegar

For the finish

- Two packages tortillas

JASON SANTOS

You may know Jason Santos as the chef with the electric blue hair. Whether you've seen him alongside Chef Gordon Ramsey on *Hell's Kitchen*, helping people get their businesses in order on *Bar Rescue*, or on countless local and national morning shows where he delights hosts like Kelly Ripa or Al Roker with culinary treats, Chef Santos is an unabashedly funky star, not only on screen, but in the kitchens of his many restaurants in the Boston area. And in our opinion, he makes the best damn chicken and waffles you'll ever have.

Chef Santos was born and raised in Melrose, Massachusetts, and often jokes that he came out of the womb making aioli. As a kid, he took notes watching Julia Child on TV and tried out recipes while most kids were on the playground. His passion for cooking continued when he graduated from Newbury College's culinary arts program, moved on to work for Andy Husbands at Tremont 647 for six years, and in 2005 became the executive chef at Gargoyles on the Square.

It was when Chef Santos ventured out on his own as a chef/owner that we and the city really took notice of his style and extreme inventiveness. He is always trying to think of creative and colorful ways to present his food with delicious results. Each of his restaurants feature crazily creative cocktails, and his ability to create a distinct vibe is unparalleled.

We were there when he opened his first Buttermilk & Bourbon on Commonwealth Avenue, and not only was the food paying deep respect to New Orleans, we felt Jason had physically brought Louisiana to Massachusetts. There were murals with giant skulls, church pews that had been brought in as part of the furniture, and beignets that could have come straight out of Café du Monde.

Chef Santos never feels boxed in by any type of cuisine, bringing his skill and unique takes to all types of food. At Citrus & Salt, he's delivered coastal Mexican-inspired dishes. Nash Bar & Stage on Tremont Street brings Nashville line dancing and live music to Bostonians. And Buttermilk & Bourbon on Comm Ave. and in Watertown's Arsenal Yards gives the city the opportunity to let the good times roll in New Orleans fashion.

When he isn't writing successful cookbooks, supporting non-profits such as Share Our Strength's Operation Frontline, spending time with his wife and adorable daughter, running restaurants, or starring on TV, he finds time to dye his own hair trademark blue.

CHICKEN AND WAFFLE TACOS WITH LIME SYRUP, WATERMELON PICO DE GALLO, AND AVOCADO BUTTER

Serves 8

This is one of the coolest presentations you will find. Is it a taco or is it chicken and waffles? Well, it's both. It's obviously, at heart, some good southern chicken and waffles, but it comes with a Latin twist for some flair and funk.

To make the buttermilk marinade

1. Mix buttermilk and hot sauce together in a large mixing bowl and set aside.

To make the chicken dredge

1. Mix all the ingredients together and set aside.

To make the chicken

1. Place cleaned chicken strips into the buttermilk marinade for a minimum of 4 hours, but soaking them overnight is best.

2. Once ready, remove chicken from marinade and toss in fry dredge until completely coated.

3. In either a medium-size pot or a cast-iron pan, heat canola oil to 350°F. Carefully add chicken to oil and cook for 10 to 12 minutes. When done remove chicken from oil and season with salt and pepper.

To make the lime syrup

1. Bring agave syrup to a boil and remove from heat.

2. Add remaining ingredients and keep warm.

To make the avocado butter

1. Add avocado pulp, lime juice, garlic, and cumin to a food processor and puree until smooth.

2. Add in butter and puree to combine.

3. Season with salt and pepper.

4. Refrigerate for up to a week or freeze until you are ready to use.

For the buttermilk marinade

1 cup buttermilk

1 tablespoon crystal hot sauce

For the chicken dredge

1 tablespoon lemon pepper

1 tablespoon granulated garlic powder

1 teaspoon old bay seasoning

1/2 teaspoon crushed red pepper flakes

1/2 teaspoon dried oregano

2 cups masa harina flour

2 cups all-purpose flour

1/2 teaspoon salt

1 teaspoon ground black pepper

1/4 teaspoon cayenne pepper

For the chicken

4 large, boneless, skinless chicken thighs, trimmed of excess fat and cut in half lengthwise

Canola oil for frying

Salt, to taste

Black pepper, to taste

For the lime syrup

1 cup agave syrup

1/2 tablespoon Asian chile sambal paste

To make the watermelon pico de gallo

1. Combine all ingredients and season.

To make the waffles

1. Preheat waffle according to the manufacturer's settings.

2. Sift together the flour, cornmeal, sugar, baking powder, and salt in a bowl.

3. In a separate bowl, whisk together the bourbon, milk, buttermilk, and eggs.

4. Pour bourbon mixture over the dry ingredients and stir until halfway combined.

5. Pour in the melted butter and continue mixing very gently until combined.

6. Scoop the batter into your waffle iron in batches and cook according to its directions (lean toward the waffles being a little deep golden and crisp).

7. Remove from iron, fold waffle, and place in taco stand.

To finish

1. Top waffle taco with 2 strips of fried chicken and a scoop of watermelon pico de gallo. Garnish with cilantro, and serve with lime wedges, lime syrup, and avocado butter. Serve immediately.

Zest and juice of 1 lime
Pinch of smoked salt

For the avocado butter

1/2 cup fresh avocado pulp
1 tablespoon lime juice
1 garlic clove, minced
1/2 teaspoon ground cumin
8 tablespoons (1 stick) butter, softened
Salt, to taste
Black pepper, to taste

For the watermelon pico de gallo

1 cup peeled, small-diced watermelon
1/4 cup minced red onion
1 tablespoon lime juice
1 tablespoon minced cilantro
1 teaspoon minced jalapeño
Salt, to taste
Black pepper, to taste

For the waffles

1 cup all-purpose flour
1/2 cup blue cornmeal
3 tablespoons sugar
1/2 tablespoon baking powder
1/2 teaspoon salt
1 tablespoon bourbon
1/2 cup milk
1/2 cup buttermilk
2 eggs
3 tablespoons butter, melted

For the finish

Cilantro sprigs
Lime wedges

CHRIS HIMMEL AND ROBERT SISCA

Pictured: Chef Robert Sisca

For forty years, Grill 23 & Bar has been the steakhouse in Boston that guests flock to for exceptional service, generously poured chilled martinis, exquisite cuts of meat, and an internationally recognized and award-winning wine program like no other.

Grill 23 & Bar in the Back Bay is a cornerstone of fine dining in the city and where Billy often brings friends and family. We've been covering the Himmel Hospitality Group's commitment to dining at its finest for years. Second-generation restaurateur Chris Himmel is carrying on his family's life work with care. We have no doubt Grill 23 & Bar will be around for decades to come.

Chef Robert Sisca (photographed here), culinary director and partner of the Himmel Hospitality Group restaurants that include Bistro du Midi, The Banks Seafood and Steak, and Harvest, says the key to Grill 23's success is consistency. He credits much of this consistency in quality to the staff, some of whom have been working at Grill 23 & Bar for thirty years. The same butchers have mastered their craft over twenty years, the same prep cooks know exactly how guests like their potatoes whipped, and the servers know what standards are expected at such a reputable establishment.

Grill 23 & Bar's success is also due to the partnership of Chris Himmel and Chef Robert, which is built on a foundation of respect. Himmel grew up helping at his family's Grill 23 restaurant, learning the ins and outs of how to treat guests with the utmost care from those closest to him. With an education at Cornell's School of Hotel Administration, and experience gained from working under Chefs Danny Meyer and Thomas Keller, he felt prepared to come home and continue his family's legacy.

Chef Sisca is also all about family legacy. His mother has been, and continues to be, an inspiration to him. She passed down the art of cooking authentic Italian cuisine to Chef Sisca the same way her mother passed it on to her. Those cherished recipes that have been preserved over time have found a special place in Chef Sisca's culinary repertoire. Memories of his mother's love of cooking and teaching all that she learned to her son can be seen in all of Chef Sisca's menus.

At the French Bistro du Midi overlooking the Public Garden, and at The Banks Seafood and Steak in Back Bay, we can also see the influence of Chef Sisca's culinary mentor, Chef Eric Ripert. Chef Sisca says that working under Chef Ripert's guidance was like getting a master's degree in seafood preparation. He learned far more than cooking from his mentor, he learned everything that goes into managing a restaurant and the people working there.

Grill 23 serves a one-hundred-day aged, 18-ounce rib eye that is a timeless classic. The master sommeliers on hand at the restaurant are happy to select the right wine to go with it. As one of the few restaurants in the world that has received the Wine Spectator Grand Award, Grill 23 has a rare and extensive wine cellar. In another forty years, we doubt guests will even be able to make a dent in that list, but we know those lucky enough to dine at Grill 23 are more than willing to try.

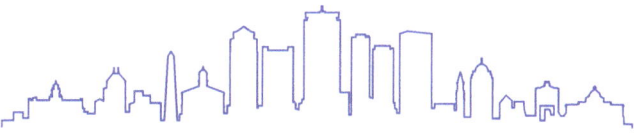

RIBEYE, BUTTER-POACHED LOBSTER, CARAMELIZED ONIONS, AND WATERCRESS

Serves 2

Just like Chris Himmel and Chef Robert Sisca, this surf and turf recipe is an excellent combination—the best of both worlds on one plate.

To make the caramelized onions

1. Place sliced onions in Dutch oven (or round pot) with canola oil on low heat. Season with salt and pepper. Cover with lid to steam onions to help create some liquid. Once onions are soft, turn heat up with lid off and caramelize them for about 15 minutes until desired color is achieved. Finish with soy sauce (or tamari), balsamic vinegar, and honey after onions have turned golden brown.

To make the butter-poached lobster

1. Bring 1 inch of water to a boil in a large pot or deep skillet with a tight-fitting lid. Place a steamer basket over water.

2. Place tails, cut-side up, in the basket. Cover and steam until meat is just opaque and very plump, about 5 to 6 minutes. Do not overcook or meat will begin to shrink and dry out.

To make the rib eye

1. Remove steaks from fridge and let temper for 20 minutes prior to cooking.

1. Preheat grill to high.

2. Season steaks with salt and pepper. The thicker the steak, the more salt and pepper you will need.

3. Place steaks on preheated grill and cook until desired internal temperature is reached. Depending on thickness, medium rare will be around 125°F to 130°F, approximately 5 minutes on each side. Rest steak for 5 to 10 minutes before slicing. **Note:** Steaks will continue to cook 5 to 10 degrees more after being pulled off the grill.

To finish

1. Top rib eyes with a scoop of caramelized onions and a side of lobster. Garnish with watercress.

For the caramelized onions

- 1 pounds onions, sliced
- 3 tablespoons canola oil
- 1 teaspoon salt
- 1 teaspoon black pepper
- 2 tablespoons soy sauce or gluten-free tamari
- 2 tablespoons balsamic vinegar
- 1/4 teaspoon honey

For the butter-poached lobster

- 2 raw shelled lobster tails

For the rib eye

- 2 18-ounce prime rib eyes (Brandt is Chef Sisca's choice)
- Salt, to taste
- Black pepper, to taste

For the finish

- 4 cups watercress, rinsed and dried

CHEF'S TIP: You never want to cook anything directly from fridge. Allow your steak to temper for around 20 minutes before cooking. This will allow it to cook more evenly.

NANCY AND TIM CUSHMAN

Some might not know this, but Ryan Reynolds and Blake Lively fell in love while Ryan was on a film shoot in our great city. Their favorite restaurant? o ya, a Japanese-inspired restaurant that put exemplary sushi on the map in Boston and in the US. Blake commented on Ryan's glowing Instagram post about the restaurant with, "If it weren't for this place. We wouldn't be together. No joke. No restaurant means more to us."

That means this beloved celebrity couple may not exist were it not for one of *our* favorite couples, Tim and Nancy Cushman, owners of o ya, Hojoko, gogoya, and bianca to name a few in their ever-expanding culinary empire.

Their restaurant group, Cushman Concepts, has tasty places to dine in California and New York, but we'll be focusing on where it all started, right here in Boston. Tim originally began his career as a musician, going to Berklee College of Music, where he studied jazz and classical guitar. When he moved to California to pursue his craft, he found work in restaurant kitchens to pay the bills. There, he was mentored by chefs who showed him how to create global menus of all types of cuisine.

Tim discovered that he wanted to put his creative energy toward the culinary arts and wound up working in kitchens all over the world, including in Japan, Thailand, Germany, Italy, Mexico, Taiwan, and Hong Kong.

It was when he moved to Chicago that he met his future business partner, and partner in all things, Nancy. She had a successful career in advertising where, much like Tim, she also enjoyed mixing creativity with business. On one of their first dates, Tim introduced Nancy to sake, which started a lifelong passion for the beverage for Nancy. She has been to Japan many times to study the art of sake and is one of the few people in the world to be certified in the Advanced Sake Professional Course.

When the couple opened their first restaurant, o ya, the awards and recognition came flooding in. There was nowhere in Boston at that time where one could have a very high-end, authentic, and atmospheric Japanese cuisine experience, and diners took notice. In 2008, *New York Times* critic Frank Bruni named o ya the number-one new restaurant in the US, and *Food & Wine* magazine named it one of the top-ten new restaurants in the world. Since then, o ya has always had a wait list, and Chef Tim Cushman has gone on to become a James Beard Award winner.

We have memories of the couple helping with benefits for non-profits like Rosie's Place. We also have memories of us being terrified of landing on the wasabi-loaded piece of sushi on the Wasabi Roulette Wheel at Hojoko in Fenway and of Billy trying to cook a Hojoko wagyu burger with Tim in studio and just getting smoke in his eyes for what felt like hours. Both of us had tears in our eyes, one from the smoke, the other from laughing so hard off camera.

HOJOKO WASABI ROULETTE SUSHI

Serves 6

The roulette wheel at Hojoko is a new tradition that's a lot of fun, but beware the sushi piece that holds the wasabi bomb! The sushi pieces are placed individually on a lazy Susan and no one knows where the wasabi loaded piece is . . . or who will land on it. Take this challenge on at home and good luck!

For the negihama mix

1. Combine all ingredients in a mixing bowl and stir with a spatula to combine. Set aside until ready to make the sushi roll.

To make the sushi

1. Cut the nori sheet in half widthwise so you have two even squares. Stack the squares on top of each other and cut each piece into thirds so you have six rectangular strips that are a little bigger than 4- x 1-inch each.

2. Divide sushi rice into 6 equal portions and shape into 3/4-inch-wide cylinders that are about 1 inch tall.

3. Dab a little wasabi paste on each cylinder of sushi rice, except for one that will have the "wasabi bomb."

4. Wrap the nori strips around the cylinder so it wraps around the rice. For the piece that has the "wasabi bomb," gently push the rice down and create a divot with your thumb so that 1/2 teaspoon or so of wasabi will fit.

5. Divide the negihama mix to 1 tablespoon balls and roll between your hands so they are smooth. Place one ball on top of each piece of sushi rice. Garnish with toasted sesame seeds, toasted sesame oil, and fried garlic.

6. Serve with soy sauce and gari (pickled ginger).

For the negihama mix

- 4 ounces yellowtail Hamachi (or any sushi-grade fish), finely chopped
- 1½ tablespoon minced scallions
- 1/2 tablespoon minced shiso leaf
- 1/2 tablespoon soy sauce

For the sushi

- 1 nori sheet
- 1/2 cup vinegared sushi rice
- Prepared wasabi paste, as needed
- 6 tablespoons negihama mix
- 1/8 teaspoon toasted sesame seeds
- 1/8 teaspoon toasted sesame oil
- 1/8 teaspoon fried garlic

CHEF'S TIP: Plate the sushi pieces in a circular pattern on a round plate that spins to randomize and make things fun! Good luck!

CHEF'S TIP: This recipe calls for Hamachi, but many other fishes would work here as well, including tuna (toro), Kanpachi, hiramasa, etc.

FENWAY PARK

What else can be said about one of the jewels of a huge sports town? It's a beacon for Red Sox fans as one of the oldest ballparks in Major League Baseball that's been home to the team since 1912, but it's a lot more than that. Sure, there's nothing quite like being at a game, singing with the crowd to Neil Diamond's "Sweet Caroline" (even if we sometimes have trouble staying in tune) at the bottom of the eighth inning, but there's also nothing like being in the Fenway area even when the Sox aren't playing. The neighborhood hosts some of our favorite restaurants, such as Sweet Cheeks Q, Hojoko, and Eastern Standard Kitchen.

Photo courtesy of Jenny Johnson

Fenway has hosted a ton of events like hockey games, soccer matches, and incredible concerts. The stadium also hosted the country's largest naturalization ceremony, with five thousand new American citizens fulfilling their dreams in a place where making dreams come true is just another day at the park.

Fenway Park became an even more special place to us when we joined the NESN family. Jenny's friendship with Red Sox Chairman Tom Werner, coupled with his esteemed background in TV production, paved the way for our involvement with NESN. We've gotten to know many of the Red Sox players personally and have interviewed them over the years. They trust us to tell their stories because we ask them questions that go beyond baseball. After all, in Fenway Park and at NESN, we're all on the same team.

ASIA MEI

Moonshine 152 in South Boston is like a modern-day *Cheers*, a neighborhood hub where people in the community can gather. The Sam Malone of this place is Asia Mei.

Like Sam Malone, she's the heart of the place, front and center, greeting guests, firing up the line in the kitchen, bussing tables, creating the bright and colorful paintings that adorn the walls, and doing all of it with an effervescence.

Like the fictional Sam Malone, who was a former Red Sox player, Mei has a wild past. During college summers, she worked as a stuntwoman doing martial arts in Hollywood films!

She's a jack-of-all trades who's good at everything; someone whose warmth makes residents want to return to Moonshine whenever they need to feel welcomed.

How did she go from martial arts—and a college education in economics and biology—to the restaurant business?

After graduating from Boston College, she found a job at Hamersley's Bistro where she was mentored by the great chef Gordon Hamersley. Chef Hamersley is an absolute legend in the industry. A protégé of Julia Child, an expert in French cuisine and technique, he's also one of the kindest and most welcoming chefs we've come across. Chef Mei honed her skills as his sous chef for four years and now embodies not only Chef Hamersley's precision and love of New England ingredients but also his warmth, generosity, and leadership.

Chef Mei worked at other restaurants, including Sibling Rivalry, Franklin Southie, and Sam's on the Waterfront, as well as doing a stint as head chef at Whole Foods, but it was at her own restaurant where she was able to focus her talent and vision to create the perfect neighborhood spot.

The menu at Moonshine 152 is eclectic and comforting, pushes boundaries, always features something new based on the season, and satisfies cravings we didn't know we had. Dishes like Throwback Korean BBQ Tacos, Chef Asia's Famous Vegetarian Mushroom Tofu Burger, Louisiana-Braised Rabbit Pasta, Spicy Lamb Meatballs (featured on *Chopped*), and Mama Mei's Famous Dirty Fried Rice are just a few of the favorites. But it isn't just the food that has created such a devoted following. People love Chef Mei—for good reason.

When the pandemic caused Moonshine 152 to shut down, Chef Mei rose to the occasion to help take care of her staff and the community. She had a fire sale and got rid of everything in the restaurant from patio umbrellas to plates; auctioned off her paintings, those painted by her as well as those of artist friends who donated their pieces; and worked as a private chef in people's homes—all the money she raised was given to her staff.

She also partnered with the American Red Cross and set up a blood drive in her closed restaurant, with the community coming out in droves. Chef Asia Mei shows up for community, and the community does the same for her.

It's this kind of leadership, as well as an open viral letter to the governor and mayor about how the pandemic was impacting small businesses, that earned her a Greater Boston Chamber of Commerce Small Business CEO Leadership Award.

We highly recommend visiting Moonshine 152 for brunch on the weekend. Soon enough, Chef Mei might know your name.

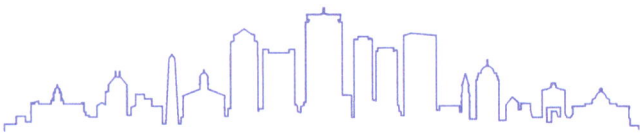

GOOD LUCK LUMPIA WITH SHRIMP AND GROUND TURKEY FILLING

Makes 20

Shrimp and ground turkey lumpia is essentially the Filipino version of a crispy spring roll, which is otherwise found in many Asian cultures, including Japanese, Chinese, and Thai. A ubiquitous and delightfully appealing appetizer, Good Luck Lumpia showcases the delicious combination of savory shrimp and seasoned ground turkey encased in thin spring roll wrappers. This is the "fancy" version to celebrate all the good luck we wish for everyone!

We take special care in this recipe to wrap seasoned ground turkey around a whole trimmed shrimp, then wrap it in the spring roll wrappers. This retains the shape of the shrimp after it is fried and offers a much more indulgent ratio of shrimp filling, allowing the whole shrimp to be enjoyed with all of its integrity intact.

Now, let's get rolling!!

To make the ground turkey filling

1. In a bowl combine all the ingredients for the ground turkey filling. Mix well, traditionally by hand or using chopsticks, in one direction. Set aside.

To make the lumpia

1. Score peeled and deveined shrimp slightly on both top and bottom sides. The scoring process helps ensure that the shrimp will retain their flat shape instead of curling up when cooked.

2. Cut your spring roll wrappers in half diagonally to form 2 large triangles per wrapper.

3. Wrap approximately 2 tablespoons ground turkey filling around the shrimp using your hands. You'll want enough to create a 1/4- to 1/2-inch layer around the shrimp. Place the filling and wrapped shrimp along the middle of the wrapper on the side where you made the diagonal cut. The tail should hang over the end of the wrapper, exposed as an open end to the lumpia. Don't worry, the open end won't be an issue when frying because the turkey filling will set as it cooks!

4. Fold the top corner down toward the shrimp. The bottom middle corner should also be folded up to seal the end of the lumpia.

For ground turkey filling

- 1 pound ground turkey
- 1 cup finely diced scallions or garlic chives
- 1 tablespoon onion powder
- 1 tablespoon finely chopped garlic
- 1 tablespoon finely chopped ginger
- 1/2 tablespoon mushroom powder
- 1 large egg
- 1/4 cup shredded carrot
- 1/2 tablespoon sugar
- 2½ tablespoons sherry wine or Shaoxing cooking wine
- 1/2 tablespoon white pepper
- 2 teaspoons kosher salt
- 2 tablespoons cornstarch

For lumpia

- 20 large shrimp (tail on, deveined and peeled)
- 1 package 8-inch spring roll wrappers
- 1 egg for egg wash
- Canola oil for frying

(Continued)

5. Fold the edges toward the middle and roll tightly. Seal with egg wash.

6. Wrap once more with the other half of the wrapper and seal again with egg wash. This creates a more secure spring roll, and once fried it will also be crispier.

7. Fry lumpia in canola oil heated to 350°F for 8 to 10 minutes until golden brown and crispy. If they pick up the color you want before the centers are cooked, feel free to finish in an oven or toaster oven for a few minutes at a time. You can always cut one in the middle to see how cooked it is, or use a probe to test the center for doneness (165°F). These are great to serve cut along the diagonal also, because it really highlights the use of the whole shrimp.

8. Serve immediately! Of course, garnish with any of your favorite dipping sauces, chopped peanuts, fresh lettuce wraps, and/or herbs!

CHEF'S TIP: Always feel free to taste test your filling by cooking off a little bit in a pan!

" **Billy:** You're going to feel lucky after tasting Chef Mei's recipe.

Jenny: We're so lucky she's in Boston, making food that brings the neighborhood together. "

PATRICIA ESTORINO

We ask many restaurateurs who come on our show why they chose to open their business. Some say they love food. Others say they enjoy nightlife.

Patricia Estorino's answer to the question has always stuck with us. She was the only person to answer, "Homesickness."

Originally from Cuba, Estorino is chef/owner of Gustazo in Cambridge and Waltham. She told us there that while she found a few Cuban eateries in Massachusetts, she was missing specific flavors and meals from her home country. After many years of cooking for herself and her family, she felt it was time to bring the Cuban cuisine she remembered and grew up on to the public. We are *very* happy she did.

Chef Estorino grew up in Havana, where she trained to be a dancer and was a ballerina with the National Dance Company of Cuba.

In 2001 she and her musician husband, Adolfo De La Vega, moved to Boston after he'd been awarded a scholarship to study music at Longy School of Music Cambridge.

Estorino continued working as a dancer and taught dance for many years, but her love of food—and her desire to share the food she loved—led her and her husband to open Gustazo Cuban Café in 2011 in the town of Belmont. The food proved so popular, and the cozy Belmont location too small to accommodate the many guests, that the couple closed the restaurant in Belmont and opened Gustazo

Cuban Kitchen and Bar on Main Street in Waltham, with a location in the Porter Square neighborhood of Cambridge not far behind.

Gustazo roughly translates to "great pleasure," and given the artistic backgrounds of Chef Estorino and her husband, everything about their restaurants is a great pleasure to the senses. The colorful wall full of Cuban movie posters, the soundtrack of salsa and Cuban jazz in the background, a bar with hard-to-find rums, the odes to Cuban art as well as a map of Cuba made out of tobacco leaves on the wall, all make guests feel like they've been transported to Havana. But it's Chef Estorino's menu that gives the greatest pleasure of all.

Her interpretations of the food she cherished are vibrant, flavorful, always changing based on the season, and always delicious. Her empanadas are *not* to be missed and every day brings a new offering. Tapas such a Ceviche, Costillas a la Guyaba (guava-glazed baby back ribs served with a pineapple and heart of palm puree with pickled beets and roasted peanuts), and Jibarito (a deconstructed Cuban sandwich over tostones) are all made for sharing. But you will want to keep everything for yourself. Some of us aren't always into sharing (cough, Jenny).

Entrees such as Ropa Vieja (which Chef Estorino told us translates to "old clothes") is actually a shredded flank steak dish in an incredible tomato sauce served with rice, black beans, and maduros. It's just one example of why Chef Estorino, with no formal training, was nominated for Best Chef Northeast by the James Beard Foundation.

We've featured Chef Estorino on our show, and while she is very humble and quick to celebrate other women in the industry, she should feel proud knowing her food is bringing Cuban culture to Boston and that she can preserve her fond memories of her grandmother's cooking for her young daughter.

EMPANDAS DE PICADILLO (GROUND BEEF EMPANADAS)

Makes about 24

Empanda comes from the Spanish word empanar, which means to wrap in bread. Chef Estorino's Beef Empanadas are comfort food wrapped in dough and memories of home.

To make the dough

1. Add dry ingredients in food processor and pulse to combine.
2. Add frozen butter cubes and pulse a few times to break down butter and coat with flour mixture.
3. Add beaten egg and milk carefully, just until the dough comes together and there is no trace of flour, do not overmix.
4. Place dough on a lightly floured surface and shape into a log approximately 10 inches in length.
5. Let dough cool in the refrigerator for about 2 hours before using.

To make the filling

1. In a large sauté pan add olive oil and garlic and sauté garlic gently over medium-low heat until garlic begins to turn golden and is very fragrant.
2. Add peppers, onions, salt, and pepper, and increase heat to medium-high.
3. Incorporate oregano, cumin, paprika, bay leaves, and beef base and continue cooking over medium-high heat, stirring frequently until vegetables are well caramelized and a fond begins to form.
4. Add wine and raise heat to high to deglaze pan.
5. Add tomato paste and water and incorporate well.
6. Reduce heat to low, cover, and cook for approximately 5 minutes.
7. Add meat to the pan, separating into small portions. Stir in vegetables and cover and cook at low heat for approximately 10 minutes, breaking up any clumps of meat.
8. Remove pan from heat, add sherry vinegar, raisins and olives if desired, let cool. Adjust seasoning as needed. Let final mix chill in the refrigerator for at least 2 hours before assembling empanadas.

(Continued)

For the dough

- 3 cups all-purpose flour
- 1/2 teaspoon table salt
- 1 teaspoon sugar
- 8 ounces salted butter, cut into 1-inch cubes and frozen
- 1 egg, beaten
- 1/2 cup milk

For the filling

- 1/4 cup olive oil
- 2 tablespoons minced garlic
- 2 large red bell peppers, diced small
- 2 yellow onions, diced small
- 2 teaspoons kosher salt
- 1/2 teaspoon freshly ground black pepper
- 2 teaspoons dried oregano
- 1/2 teaspoon cumin
- 1 teaspoon smoked spicy Spanish paprika
- 3–4 bay leaves
- 1 teaspoon beef base
- 1/4 cup white wine
- 3 tablespoons tomato paste
- 1/4 cup water
- 1 pound ground beef

To make the empanadas

1. Cut dough log into 1/4-inch-thick discs and flatten with a rolling pin to obtain discs of approximately 4 inches in diameter and 1/16 inch thick.

2. Mix egg and sugar and using a pastry brush and apply mix to the border of the discs.

3. Place one spoonful filling in the center of each disc and fold over, pressing the edges with your fingers.

4. Using a fork, press down all around the edges to seal the empanadas.

5. Brush empanada with the egg wash, making sure to cover thoroughly but lightly to prevent them from becoming too dark when baking.

6. Bake at 375°F for 20 to 30 minutes, turning the pan halfway through until golden and somewhat crispy.

1 teaspoon Vinagre de Jerez (Spanish sherry vinegar)
1/4 cup raisins (optional)
1/4 cup pimiento stuffed olives, sliced thin (optional)

For the empanadas

1 egg, beaten
1/2 teaspoon sugar

> **Billy:** Chef Estorino's food makes me feel like I'm visiting Havana.
>
> **Jenny:** And her empanadas are made with love and are a comfort food for everyone.

THANAPHON "SONG" AUTHAIPHAN

One of us (Jenny) has had a once-in-a-lifetime trip to Thailand. The other of us (Billy) would rather be on his boat than take a long flight. Luckily, there's a place close to home where we can both feel like we're visiting Bangkok. It's Mahaniyom in Brookline Village, and it's one of the best places to go and share food. Go with a bunch of friends and order everything. It'll be a night to remember.

Mahaniyom, a Thai tapas bar is the brainchild of restaurateurs Chompon "Boong" Boonak and Smuch "Top" Saikamthorn, who've been friends since they were four years old while growing up in the Phetchabun province of Thailand. Saikamthorn, who'd run a Thai restaurant in San Diego, came to Boston to study at Northeastern University. Boonak studied at Boston University, and was a long-time bartender at Shōjō in Boston's Chinatown. The two put their experience together and decided to bring the flavors they missed from their childhood to showcase Thai culture and cuisine with dishes you won't find anywhere else in Boston.

Mahaniyom roughly translates to "beloved," which is fitting for the intimate, sleek space in Brookline Village that's incredibly popular. The menu comes from Chef Thanaphon "Song" Authaiphan, who brings the memories of the meals the co-owners had in Thailand to life.

Chef Song's passion for cooking started when his father asked him to help out in the kitchen as he was preparing meals for their family. Chef Song's culinary mentor in Boston is Wongsakorn "Pap" Amorncharoenchai, a sushi chef at Fat Baby, and he credits *our* show for letting him know which restaurants to check out on his days off!

Chef Song doesn't serve an Americanized version of Thai food at Mahaniyom. He and his team whip up dishes from scratch, including Salt and Pepper Pork Cheek glazed in a secret combo of Thai spices and chilies and served with sticky rice; Massaman, housemade curry with slow-cooked beef shank, sweet potato, onions, pickled shallots, and roasted peanuts served with roti ready for dipping; and noodle staple Pad Thai that trumps any Pad Thai you've ever had.

Mahaniyom has only been open since 2020, but it's made a big impression in a short amount of time. It was Eater Boston's best new restaurant in 2021, and in 2022 received a five-star review from the *Boston Globe*. Even celebrity chef Gordon Ramsay is a big fan, having visited the restaurant and praised the team for an authentic and outstanding meal.

Mahaniyom is a fantastic place to meet up with a co-worker after work for a bite, have a second date when coffee just won't cut it, or call your friends and have a Thai getaway without having to go to Logan Airport. And you can be home in time for the Bruins game on TV. No jet lag necessary.

GREEN PAPAYA PAD THAI

Serves 1 as a main dish or 2 as a side

A dazzling blend of sweet and citrus, these noodles have a light, fresh snap to them.

To make the pad Thai sauce

1. Soak chilis in warm water for 10 to 15 minutes until soft.
2. Mix chili with white vinegar.
3. In a sauce pot over medium-high heat, combine all ingredients and cook until they dissolve. Reduce heat and simmer for 10 to 15 minutes.

To make the pad Thai

1. Heat oil in saute pan. Add shrimp and fry until they are bright pink. Remove and set them aside.
2. In the same pan, stir-fry shallots, radishes, and tofu. Add eggs and scramble.
3. Add papaya or carrots and cucumbers and fry until soft.
4. Add 6 tablespoons pad Thai sauce, Chinese chives, and bean sprouts.

To finish

1. Serve with shrimp on top of additional fresh bean sprouts and chives. Sprinkle with peanuts, chili powder, shrimp flakes, and garnish with lime slice.

CHEF'S TIP: You will have leftover pad Thai sauce, but don't worry; it can be stored in the refrigerator for up to a month.

For the pad Thai sauce

- 2 dried New Mexico chilis, seeded
- 2 tablespoons white vinegar
- 1/4 cup fish sauce
- 4 tablespoons palm sugar or brown sugar
- 1/2 cup tamarind juice

For the stir-fry

- 1/4 cup cooking oil
- 5 shrimp
- 2 tablespoons sliced shallots
- 2 tablespoons chopped sweet radishes
- 3 tablespoons extra-firm tofu (cut into 1/2-inch cubes)
- 2 large eggs
- 1½ cups shredded green papaya or shredded carrots and cucumber mixture
- 1/8 cup Chinese chives (cut into 2-inch lengths) or scallions (plus more for serving)
- 1/4 cup bean sprouts (plus more for serving)

For the garnish

- 1 tablespoon ground peanuts
- 1 teaspoon chili powder
- 1 tablespoon shrimp flakes
- 1 slice of lime

PAM AND CHRIS WILLIS

We know firsthand how popular Pammy's in Cambridge has become in a few short years. Why? Viewers were thrilled when we featured husband-and-wife restaurateur team Pam and Chef Chris Willis on our show. Also, it's not easy to get a reservation! Billy's son Alex called a few months ago from Florida and said he was doing everything he could to get a reservation at Pammy's and asked if his dad would help. A month later, Billy's *other* son, Chris, called from California and said his wife Hannah *had* to go to Pammy's.

The restaurant has a feverish cult following, and it's deserved.

Pammy's, which opened on Mass Ave. between Harvard and Central Square in 2017, serves New American– and Italian-inspired dishes. The only rules at Pammy's are that the food must be good, and the atmosphere has to make it feel like people are coming home.

Chef Chris Willis grew up on his family's farm in Sherborne, Massachusetts, learning how to prepare the animals for dinner. Pam grew up in New York City, the daughter of a restaurateur and a hotelier, and spent her after-school hours helping out by doing small tasks like folding napkins.

Chris wanted to be a drummer. Pam was trained as an actress at NYU's Tisch School of the Arts. But when they met in Nantucket as adults, it was the start of a lifelong partnership and the beginning of what would eventually become their dream to own a restaurant.

Chef Chris can be found in the kitchen of Pammy's, milling flour for the bread and pasta and preparing dishes like Lumache pasta in a bolognese with Korean gochujang sauce or Branzino served with a turnip cake, daikon radish puree, and kohlrabi relish.

Pam can often be found front of house, always fabulously dressed, greeting guests and making sure everyone in the restaurant feels like they're part of the "Pamily." The restaurant has beautiful potted plants, refurbished antiques, a giant fireplace, a communal table in the heart of the restaurant, statues, and a book nook, just in case guests want to do some reading.

Pammy's can become anything you'd like it to be based on your mood—a romantic venue for a date or a great hangout spot for friends after work. But it also feels like an extension of the couple's home, which they share with their two children down the street.

SPAGHETTI SQUASH AND BURATTA

Serves 4 to 6

At Pammy's this dish is a fan favorite as a starter but at home it can be eaten alongside chicken, pork, or even fish, or served in a larger portion as a vegetarian entree. There are so many ways to dress up the three key players (squash, burrata, and crostini), Chef Chris has included recipes for the "touches" (as they call them at the restaurant) they chose at Pammy's—chili honey and good quality olives. The curry oil is not essential (a good quality olive oil will do), but it adds an intriguing accent that is a good conversation starter.

To make the curry leaf oil

1. Put leaves and oil in a high-rimmed sauté pan.
2. Cook on maximum heat until leaves begin to fry.
3. Gently stir to ensure that all leaves become crispy and translucent.
4. Strain oil and cool immediately. This can be stored in the refrigerator for a month. This oil can also be used to make a delicious aioli!

To make Pammy's masala

1. Preheat oven to 325°F.
2. Toast all the spices, except salt and turmeric, together on a sheet pan in oven until fragrant, about 2 minutes.
3. Remove from oven, add salt, and grind them together until they are fine but not a powder. Some coarse texture should remain.
4. Combine in a bowl with the turmeric and set aside.

To make the chili honey

1. Mix all the ingredients in a small saucepan. Bring to a boil for 1 minute. Remove from heat and let come to room temperature. Strain into a jar.

To make the squash

1. Preheat oven to 375°F.
2. Carefully cut the spaghetti squash in half lengthwise. Salt the cut side of the squash liberally.
3. Put it in a pan, cut side down, with thyme or any other aromatic herbs you have on hand. Put enough water in the pan to come about 1/8 inch up the side of the squash.

For the curry leaf oil

- 6 to 8 medium-size curry leaves, de-stemmed
- 1 cup extra-virgin olive oil

For Pammy's masala

- 4 teaspoons cumin
- 2 teaspoons green cardamom seeds (husks removed)
- 3 teaspoons brown mustard seeds
- 1/2 teaspoon mace
- 1/4 teaspoon clove
- 3½ teaspoons fenugreek
- 2 teaspoons salt
- 4 teaspoons ground turmeric

For the chile honey

- 1 cup honey
- 2 tablespoons chopped lemongrass
- 1 tablespoon chopped ginger
- 1/4 teaspoon chili flakes
- 1 tablespoon aria olive oil
- 1 teaspoon salt

4. Seal tightly with aluminum foil and roast for roughly 20 minutes. The trick here is to get the "meat" tender enough so that it comes off in al dente strands when scraped with a fork.

5. In a 10-inch sauté pan, mix enough cooked spaghetti squash to fill the bottom of the pan about 1/2 inch deep. Add butter and water and cook on high heat until a thick, buttery glaze is formed. Season with salt and a good splash of white balsamic. The glazed squash will take a lot of salt. More than your doctor would recommend.

6. Cut rustic bread (preferably Pammy's pugliese) into 1/4- to 1/2-thick slices, depending on your preference. Grill the slices until they are well charred. Rub with 1 garlic clove. Douse with a generous amount of curry leaf oil.

7. Take about 1/4 teaspoon of the masala and the same amount of chili powder and scatter it on and around the toasted bread.

8. Cut one burrata ball in half and place it on top of the toast. Don't feel the need to be overly gentle. Push the cheese down so it stays put.

9. Place enough prepared spaghetti squash to perch proudly on the cheese.

10. Scatter 3 or 4 olives around the bread.

11. On top of the squash, carefully place 5 or so whole parsley leaves. They make for a striking contrast against the spaghetti squash and their bitterness is key to balancing the dish.

12. Drizzle the chili honey around the tower in 3 or 4 clockwise circles. There you have it—hot, sweet, soft, crunchy, creamy, and bitter!

For the squash and burrata

- 1 spaghetti squash
- Salt, to taste
- 5 sprigs thyme
- 3 tablespoons butter
- 1/4 cup water
- 2 tablespoons white balsamic vinegar
- Rustic bread (ciabatta or baguette)
- Garlic cloves, peeled and cut crosswise
- 1/4 teaspoon Calabrian chile powder (or other mild chile)
- 1 8-ounce burrata (Maplebrook brand is Pammy's choice)
- Pitted taggiasca olives (any good quality olive will do)
- Flat-leaf parsley

CHEF'S TIP: At Pammy's, whole chilies are toasted and ground every day, but they can be hard to come by. Dried pasilla, or something mild like it, is a good substitute.

CHEF'S TIP: Salt should be used liberally, especially with something as bland as spaghetti squash. The squash will thank you for it by singing louder and more clearly than it ever has.

A Taste of Boston

FRANK DEPASQUALE AND NELLO CACCIOPPOLI

When we think of the North End, there's one original restaurateur who always comes to mind. Frank DePasquale, the brilliant mastermind behind Bricco Ristorante & Enoteca, Umbria, Mare Oyster Bar, Aqua Pazza, Quattro, Trattoria Il Panino, and a slew of other concepts under his DePasquale Ventures banner, has made the North End one of the most coveted spots for dining out. He's built a reputation as one of the premiere nightlife and hospitality titans in the city, and he's created restaurants that give guests the experience of being in Italy without ever having to travel across the Atlantic.

Billy goes *way* back with Frankie to the third grade in East Cambridge. Frank had moved from Italy to Boston with his family and was the new kid Billy and his brothers looked out for. Frank often tells people when he's around Billy that the Costa boys saved his life, as they were his protectors from any neighborhood troublemakers.

Years later, the two would reconnect when Frank was the doorman at the hottest restaurant and nightclub in the '70s and '80s, Jason's on Clarendon Street. Frank remembered how Billy, who was then a college student at Emerson, had looked out for him when they were kids and introduced Billy to the manager. Sure enough, Billy got a part-time DJ job at Jason's. It's just one example of how much of a supportive and generous mover and shaker Frank has been and continues to be.

His first culinary venture was in 1987, when he opened a small sandwich shop called Il Panino. From there, Frank's passion for Italian food and hospitality led him to create many restaurants and entertainment experiences the city had never seen before. His restaurants have been the training ground for countless chefs and restaurateurs who continue his tradition of bringing people to the table or dance floor.

His concepts are influenced by his travels to Italy, often bringing talented chefs from there to showcase authentic Italian cuisine and culture to his guests. Umbria, a perfect example of a Frank DePasquale experience, is one of the hottest reservations in the city. The chic Hanover Street supper club boasts three floors and has one of the only rooftop lounges in the North End. It's been meticulously designed with stonework brought in from Italy and has a menu that delivers gourmet Italian flavors overseen by longtime corporate chef, Nello Caccioppoli.

Chef Caccioppoli was born and raised on the Amalfi Coast. He has overseen the menus of DePasquale Ventures for years, and his food is always impressive, especially at Umbria. There are high-end steaks aged for fifty days, coffee-crusted buffalo loin, baked stuffed lobster and the Umbria Cioppino, and artisanal pastas that will make your heart sing. Chef Caccioppoli's rich and sweet Short Rib Caramelle, as well as his Gnochetti al Cinghiale, made with wild boar braised in red wine, are otherworldly. The best way to end your meal at Umbria, before hitting the dance floor, is with the quintessential North End espresso martini.

Frank said on our show that Umbria was a dream he didn't believe could come true in the North End of Boston. With his vision, and love of people and hospitality, he makes dreams come true every night for so many in the city.

WILD BOAR

Serves 6 to 8

Wild boar is a gamey, tender meat that's not typical to find. But when you do, the search is worth it.

1. Preheat oven to 300°F.
2. Pat dry the wild boar with paper towels.
3. Lightly coat wild boar chunks with flour and 1 teaspoon each of salt and pepper.
4. In sauté pan over high heat, heat 2 tablespoons olive oil and sear the meat and transfer to an oven-safe container.
5. Add the vegetables to the sauté pan, cook for five minutes, then deglaze with red wine.
6. Add remaining ingredients, cover, and cook for another five minutes.
7. Transfer all ingredients to the dish with the wild boar, cover the container, and bake in the oven for 1½ to 2 hours or until tender.
8. Once tender carefully shred the meat with a fork and mash any tomatoes that are still whole. Serve.

2½ pounds wild boar, cut in big cubes
1/2 cup flour
Salt and pepper, to taste
2 tablespoons olive oil
2 celery stalks, diced
1 carrot, diced
1 onion, diced
3 cloves garlic, minced
3 cups red wine
3 tablespoons tomato paste
1 can (28-ounce) peeled tomatoes
1 bay leaf
2 ounces dry mushrooms

Side Dish

MEET BOSTON WITH BILLY & JENNY

Boston is a big deal, and we love to show it off. Doing so means that we set the standard for the hospitality experience, showcasing the best in eats, sleeps, and more. Telling that story to visitors on our city's behalf is Meet Boston. Formerly known as the Greater Boston Convention & Visitors Bureau, Meet Boston is devoted to making the Boston, Cambridge, and the surrounding areas accessible, inclusive, informative, and fun for everyone. Say goodbye to the tourism boards of old. This nimble, imaginative organization has been instrumental in attracting millions of people worldwide by championing our restaurants, hotels, and other attractions. Martha J. Sheridan, president and CEO of Meet Boston, leads her team in partnering with other organizations to spotlight the people, places, businesses, and events that make the Greater Boston area a top-tier global destination.

Photo by Shutterstock.com

We are proud to be one of Meet Boston's partners. After spending twenty years telling the city's culinary stories, we believed we could showcase more of what makes Boston… Boston. The stars aligned when we met Martha. A powerhouse visionary, Martha was forming Meet Boston while we were conceiving a spinoff travel-style television show focused exclusively on the Hub. Our energies converged in 2024 to create *Meet Boston with Billy & Jenny* on NESN. Much like what we had been doing with restaurants with Dining Playbook, we wanted to bring viewers through the secret side door of the city with this new program. And in order to dish on all parts of the city, we enlisted the experts to reveal aspects of Boston that often go unseen.

Enter the Meet Boston Hubsters, a talented troupe of local content creators who bring us into the unique Boston they know and love. Our Hubsters spotlight the city's hidden gems in everything from fitness and fashion to hotels and hot events. In showcasing the true diversity of the city, *Meet Boston with Billy & Jenny* echoes the overriding mission of its namesake organization. As Martha and her team say, "Boston never gets old." We couldn't agree more. While our city will always be a touchstone of American history, Boston has never rested on its laurels. Innovation propels the Hub forward. Meet Boston amplifies that spirit by sharing the ever-evolving story of our city to the broader world.

Dinner

ANA SORTUN

Calm, understated, kind, smart, and brilliantly talented.

That's how we describe James Beard Award–winning chef and restaurateur Ana Sortun.

Sortun, known for the iconic Cambridge spot Oleana, is who we think of as the gold standard for everything from designing a menu to mentorship. Anything we say about her culinary contributions feels like an understatement. When we visit Oleana we don't just enjoy a dish, we revel in an *experience*. We think of flavors we've never had before. We sit around feeling grateful that Sortun has passed her philosophies about fine dining on to so many.

A bit of history: Chef Sortun grew up in Seattle. Her first restaurant job was as a dishwasher. She went on to work in Casablanca in Harvard Square, which is when she traveled to Turkey to explore the cuisine. It was at a potluck in Gaziantep that thirty-five women brought dishes that were important to them and their culture. That's where Chef Sortun fell in love with the bright colors and flavors of the food and with spices like dried sumac and cumin mixed with cinnamon.

The voyage inspired her to open Oleana—her full first name—in 2001. The restaurant was on a seemingly unimportant square in Cambridge, which was Sortun's first big statement, as far as we're concerned. High-end meals didn't have to be found in the center of town.

Within months, people flocked there. It was impossible to get a table.

To this day, you have to make reservations well in advance to sit on Sortun's beautiful patio, which feels otherworldly. Guests escape there, trying everything from Lamb and Eggplant Moussaka to Baked Alaska.

Chef Sortun is someone Jenny texts whenever she's worried about the future of food and where to find locally sourced dairy products or produce. She's always able to offer insight, as she has been all about farm-to-table at her restaurants long before it was a fad. Her commitment to farm-to-table is a passion shared with her husband, Chris Kurth, who owns Siena Farms and provides Chef Sortun with the freshest of ingredients. The farm means so much to them, it shares the same name with their beautiful daughter, Siena.

Chef Sortun is humble with us, but we must mention that she won the James Beard Award for Best Chef Northeast in 2005 and has been a semi-finalist and finalist in other categories *multiple times*.

Just as important is her contribution to the careers of others and the way she's changed the food scene across Cambridge. She's a co-owner of Sarma and Sofra, boosting the talents of Cassie Piuma at Sarma and Maura Kilpatrick at Sofra.

An award we think is just as awesome is her Women Who Give Award from Women's Lunch Place, a day shelter for women experiencing poverty and homelessness. Sortun gets her flowers for her culinary achievements frequently, but we want to note that we think of her as one of the most generous chefs in the city. Generous with her talent, her platform, and her time.

She's one of the people who makes dining here so special, in taste and in spirit.

TOPIK

Makes 12 topik

Armenians serve this meze during Lent because the flavors are so rich from spices, nuts, and dried fruit that you do not need meat. The combination of tahini and chickpeas makes a complete protein. Topik is delicious spread on bread and served with sliced radishes.

To make the tahini sauce

1. Place everything in a blender and blend until very smooth and creamy. Season with more salt if needed.

To make the hummus

1. In a large pot, cook the chickpeas in plenty of water (at least 6 cups) for about 45 minutes until very tender. Drain the chickpeas and puree them in a food processor until they are as smooth as possible.

2. Add 2 tablespoons olive oil and continue to process until very smooth. Place chickpeas in a mixing bowl and fold in riced potato. You should have equal amounts of both. Season with salt to taste; set aside.

3. Saute leeks in the remaining 2 tablespoons olive oil until very soft, jam-like. Add 2 tablespoons water after they have cooked for a few minutes to steam them and help them soften. Continue to cook until the water is gone.

4. When leeks are soft, drain them if needed and place in a mixing bowl. Stir in the currants, spices, pinenuts, and tahini. Cool.

To make the topik

1. Tear sheets of plastic wrap about 8 inches wide and lay down 4 at a time on a clean counter.

2. Scoop hummus into the middle of each wrap and flatten it with your fingers and palm into a round even circle about 1/4 to 1/2 inch thick.

3. Add 3 tablespoons of filling to the center, and using the plastic wrap to help you, roll up the sides around the filling and then twist the top of the plastic wrap to form a smooth ball.

4. Keep at room temp until ready to serve.

To finish

1. Unwrap the topik and turn onto a plate. Serve with tahini sauce and radishes.

For the tahini sauce

1 cup tahini, preferably Soom brand

1 tablespoon ground cumin

1 tablespoon fresh squeezed lemon juice

1 teaspoon finely minced garlic

2 teaspoons kosher salt, plus more to taste if needed

1 cup water with ice

For the hummus

1¼ cups chickpeas, soaked overnight and drained

4 tablespoons extra-virgin olive oil, divided

3 baking potatoes—peeled, boiled, and riced to yield 3 cups

For the filling

4 cups finely chopped leeks, mostly the white part, washed well (approximately 4 leeks)

4 tablespoons currants

1 teaspoon chopped garlic

1½ teaspoons ground cinnamon

3/4 teaspoon ground allspice

1 teaspoon ground cumin

1/2 teaspoon maras chiles

4 tablespoons pine nuts, lightly toasted

4 tablespoons tahini, Soom brand preferred

For the finish

Sliced radishes, for garnish

KRISTIN CANTY AND CHARLIE FOSTER

Before you sit down to take in the breathtaking panoramic views of the Boston Harbor from the elegant dining room or patio of Woods Hill Pier 4, make sure you let your server know you'll be starting with the Crispy Lamb Ribs. We're surprised Executive Chef Charlie Foster gave us the recipe. It's unusual to see lamb ribs on a menu, and these, in particular, are divine.

But we are reminded that Chef Foster is generous—and interested in connecting people. He wants the readers of this book to use the lamb recipe as inspiration to start a relationship with their local butcher.

This is part of the Woods Hill philosophy involving sustainability. If people better understand how to use all of an animal, there's less waste—and better business on all sides.

Owner Kristin Canty began Woods Hill after she produced and directed a documentary called *Farmageddon*—which was about threatened farmers and the health benefits of eating dairy and meat that comes straight from the animal. She was coming from the perspective of a parent who has a child with allergies and asthma and wanted to know the truth about how her child could eat in better health.

Canty went on to open the Farm at Woods Hill, a gorgeous 260-acre farm in Bath, New Hampshire, that raises and supplies the food for her three restaurants: Woods Hill Table and Adelita in Concord, Massachusetts, and Woods Hill Pier 4 in the Seaport.

Canty hired executive chef Charlie Foster to bring the bounty of her farm to guests in creative and delicious ways. A Foxboro native who studied journalism at Northeastern University, Chef Foster had a resume that included being the private chef for the Guinness family—yes, of Guinness beer fame—and working in kitchens at Michelin-starred In De Wulf in Belgium and Restaurant Frantzen in Sweden.

Chef Foster has learned to make incredible use of the bounty of ingredients he gets from the Farm at Woods Hill. After the lamb ribs, be sure to try the Made-to-Order Burrata, as well as the New England Raw Cheeses, the Dry-Aged Woods Hill Farm Duck Breast, and the Sunflower Risotto with artichoke, pickled sweet potato, oyster mushrooms, and crucolo cheese.

If you're feeling nostalgic for Anthony's Pier 4, which was a Boston institution, order the Lobster Popover. It's Chef Foster's tribute to the restaurant that came before Woods Hill Pier 4, and the popovers taste just like we remembered!

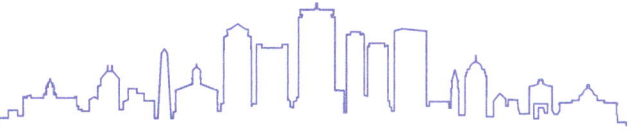

CRISPY LAMB RIBS

Serves 4

Chef Foster wants guests to have a relationship with all the offerings at their local butcher shop. These lamb ribs are not to be missed.

To cure the lamb ribs

1. Combine salt, sugar, spices, and herbs in a bowl and mix.
2. Lightly dust ribs with cure salt and let sit overnight.

To cook the lamb ribs

1. Preheat oven to 300°F.
2. Rinse lamb ribs under cold water to remove cure. Pat dry with towel.
3. Place in oven-safe dish and cover with organic sunflower oil. Cover with lid, place in oven, and cook for 2 to 3 hours until meat is tender and rib bones can be wiggled out without too much effort.
4. Remove ribs from fat and cool on rack.
5. When cooled, slice ribs into 1 or 2 bone sections, depending on the thickness of the rib.

To make the glaze

1. Combine vinegar and sugar in a sauce pot and cook over medium heat. Reduce the mixture until it starts to thicken and the sugars just start to caramelize, about 30 minutes.
2. Add shallots, bay leaves, and salt. Cook, stirring, until the water in the shallots evaporates, about 3 minutes.
3. Whisk in urfa pepper and red wine very carefully, as to not get splattered, and cook for 10 minutes so the alcohol evaporates.

To make the crispy bits

1. Heat a thin layer of salt in a cast-iron skillet over high heat. Shake the pan to ensure the salt is heating evenly.
2. Add the wild rice at once and rapidly shake the pan to evenly distribute the rice. It should take 3 to 4 minutes of heating before the rice reaches the correct temperature.
3. The rice should start to pop like popcorn. It is important that the rice explodes and turns a light brown color. If it chars and turns black, the salt

For the lamb ribs

- 1/3 cup salt
- 1 tablespoon sugar
- 1 tablespoon black peppercorns
- 1 tablespoon coriander seeds
- 1 tablespoon fennel seeds
- 1 fresh bay leaf, snipped with scissors into thin strips
- 6 thyme sprigs, snipped with scissors into pieces
- 5 pounds local, pasture-raised lamb ribs
- About 6 to 8 cups sunflower oil, enough to cover lamb in vessel

For the glaze

- 2 cups red wine vinegar
- 2 cups organic cane sugar
- 3 tablespoons minced shallots
- 2 fresh bay leaves
- 1 teaspoon salt
- 3 teaspoons urfa pepper
- 1/3 cup red wine

For the crispy bits

- 1 teaspoon salt, plus more to taste
- 3/4 cup wild rice
- Canola oil
- 1 bunch mint leaves

(Continued)

was too hot and it is burnt. If nothing happens at all, the salt was not hot enough and you need to start over again. It should only take 30 seconds.

4. Heat oil to about 375°F in a tall-sided pot, making sure the oil is at least 6 inches below the top of the pot. Add garlic and stir with a long whisk, being careful not to burn your hand with the steam that will be released.

5. When the garlic achieves a light brown color, strain the garlic from the oil and immediately spread the garlic out on some paper towels to remove excess oil.

6. Season with salt and let crisp up as it reaches room temperature.

7. Gently toast sesame seeds over medium heat until fragrant and lightly browned.

8. Combine the garlic, rice, and sesame seeds.

To prepare torn herbs

1. With your hands, tear the cilantro leaves (leaving some stem attached) and mint leaves. Mix together and keep fresh under some lightly moistened paper towels.

To finish

1. Heat some of the lamb confit oil up to 365°F in a tall-sided pot.

2. Add lamb ribs to the pot, in batches, to avoid overcrowding the pot and cooling the oil down too much. Gently stir lamb ribs as they are in the oil and fry for 2 to 3 minutes until crisp and brown.

3. Remove ribs from the oil, lightly salt, and toss in a bowl with the already warm urfa glaze. If the glaze is cold, it will be impossible to mix with the ribs easily, it is important the glaze is preheated before tossing with the ribs.

4. Stack the ribs on a plate and intersperse the layers with the torn herbs and a generous helping of the crispy bits.

5. Eat while hot.

NOTE: Do not substitute for rack of lamb, you will find lamb from a local butcher and probably in the spring so make sure you order in advance.

---

1 head of garlic, cloves separated and skin removed, smashed and diced small

2 tablespoons sesame seeds

For the torn herbs

1 bunch cilantro

Side Dish

THE FOOD PROJECT

When reflecting on the legacy we aim to create by sharing the stories of those shaping Boston's culinary landscape, we think about what the story of food will look like in the future. We think it is in good hands with the young leaders at The Food Project, a nationally acclaimed non-profit dedicated to educating and empowering youth on the intricacies of food sourcing, community support, and sustainability through hands-on farming.

Each year, The Food Project employs 140 teens to work on seventy acres of suburban and urban farmland. They learn how things grow, how to run a business by selling what they've grown at CSAs and farmers' markets, how to be of service by giving the food they've cultivated to local hunger relief organizations, and how to become leaders on the forefront of food accessibility.

The Food Project also has initiatives like Build-a-Garden that support low-to moderate income households in Mattapan, Dorchester, and Roxbury. The young teens build raised-bed gardens, lead workshops, and provide ongoing support to community members keen on growing their own food at the organization's Dudley Greenhouse.

Since 1991, The Food Project has graduated 1,800 youth who have been responsible for growing five million pounds of produce, given 100,000 hours of service to local hunger relief organizations, and built over 1,400 raised-bed gardens. It's been an honor to feature these leaders of tomorrow on our show, and we can't wait to see how their gardens continue to grow.

Photo courtesy of The Food Project

KAREN AKUNOWICZ

Her presence, her passion, and her pasta are just a few of the things that always make Chef Karen Akunowicz stand out as one of Boston's favorite restaurateurs and one of our favorite people. We knew well before *Marie Claire* magazine named her one of the "21 Badass Women Changing the Food World" just how badass she was, and is. Her knife skills, her pink hair, her tattoos, and her ability to bench press like a body builder all fit the bill for badass. But she changes the food world with her imagination, her talent, her hard work, and her kindness.

The vivacious chef-owner of Fox & the Knife Enoteca and Restaurant in the South End and the nearby Bar Volpe Ristorante & Pastificio began her hospitality career as a teenage server at a diner in her home state of New Jersey. She graduated from UMASS Amherst and had plans to get a master's degree in social work, but instead went to the Cambridge School of Culinary Arts.

From there, she gained experience by working in the kitchens of places such as Ten Tables in Jamaica Plain and Michael Schlow and Christopher Myers's Via Matta in Back Bay. She moved to Italy and made pasta at an osteria with elderly ladies and worked as a Chef at L'Avion blu Enoteca before coming back to Boston to work as Ana Sortun's sous chef at Oleana in Cambridge. But it was during her seven years as Executive Chef at Myers + Chang where high praise and national attention came her way.

Her work at Myers + Chang earned her a James Beard Award for Best Chef: Northeast, and she co-authored *Myers + Chang at Home* with mentor Joanne Chang. She also became a TV star during her many *Top Chef* and *Beat Bobby Flay* appearances, where audiences all over the world saw what we see—a funny, sweet, brilliant, and thoughtful chef who knows her stuff!

When Chef Akunowicz took a leap to start her own restaurant based on her time in Modena, Italy, everyone in the Boston culinary scene knew her talents would ensure success, and they have. Italian food is her sweet spot, and when Fox & the Knife Enoteca opened, *Food & Wine* magazine called it "An Instant Classic." In 2020, the James Beard Foundation did one better and named it a finalist for Best New Restaurant in America. Chef Akunowicz continues to travel to Italy to make sure her food is as authentic as possible.

She's been called "Boston's Queen of Pasta," and with dishes like her rich Raviolo Carbonara at Fox & the Knife or the handmade Orecchiette served with broccoli rabe, coriander, and lamb ragu at Bar Volpe, it's a title she's earned. Her reign expanded with her Fox Pasta company, which ships her handmade pasta and sauces around the country.

Chef Akunowicz is always a pleasure to be around and is one of the handful of people with incredible influence in the culinary conversations having to do with Massachusetts and New England. The Massachusetts Restaurant Association awarded her the Executive Chef of the Year award in 2022, not only for her exceptional talent in her kitchens, but for her advocacy and philanthropical work as a No Kid Hungry Chef working with the Share Our Strength organization to help food-insecure children.

The author of *Crave: Bold Recipes that Make You Want Seconds* is a rare combination of vibrancy, warmth, passion, and conviction. Every culinary event we've needed her for she's been there, and she owns the camera whenever we've asked her to be on our show. She and her wonderful spouse now have a toddler daughter, and we know Chef Akunowicz will feed her with love as she's done for so many diners in the Boston area.

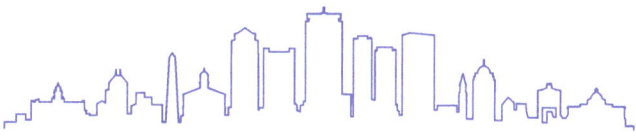

ORECCHIETTE CON CIME DI RAPA

Serves 2 (can easily be doubled for 4)

This recipe always brings me so much joy to make, and to teach. It not only comes together quickly but it is a no-fail pasta dough recipe. If you only ever learn how to make one pasta dough, this should be it. It's a great recipe to have in your back pocket!

Orecchiette is a rustic pasta from Apulia, the technique handed down from generation to generation. The dough only needs four ingredients, only takes a half hour to rest, and can be used to make various shapes.

You can always use boxed pasta in a pinch!

For the dough
- 1 cup semolina
- 3/4 cup flour
- 1 teaspoon salt
- 3/4 cup water

For the Cime di Rapa
- 1/4 cup olive oil
- 1 teaspoon kosher salt
- 2 cloves of garlic, sliced
- 1/2 teaspoon ground black pepper
- 1/2 teaspoon crushed red pepper flakes
- 1/2 cup crumbled sweet Italian sausage (or sausage of your choosing)
- 1/2 cup chicken stock (you can substitute water if you would like)
- 1/2 bunch of Broccoli rabe, chopped bite size
- 1/4 cup cooked chickpeas
- 1 tablespoon unsalted butter
- 1/4 cup pecorino sardo

To make the dough

1. Combine both flours and the salt in a medium-size mixing bowl and mix well.

2. Make a well in the middle and slowly incorporate the water with a fork. When the dough starts to come together, turn out onto a table and start to knead together until it is smooth and elastic. Cover with a tea towel or plastic wrap and rest for an hour. This dough can be made the day before and rested in the fridge overnight.

3. Once the dough is rested cut a small chunk off and roll it into a "snake" with your palms and base of your fingers. Using a bench scraper, cut little pieces off, trying to make them as uniform as possible. From here you can make orecchiette, trofie, or any short hand-rolled semolina pasta.

To complete the dish

1. Place a large pot of water on the stove to boil (about a gallon) and salt so it tastes like the ocean.

2. Place a flat-bottomed sauté pan on the stove and add olive oil to the cold pan. Turn heat up to medium and add sliced garlic. When garlic starts to "dance," add salt, pepper, and red pepper flakes, and swirl the olive oil in the pan.

3. As the garlic starts to brown, add sausage and press down with the back of a spoon. Brown the sausage for about 1 minute and then add the chicken stock to finish cooking the sausage. Turn the heat down to low and simmer for about 1 minute.

(Continued)

4. Drop 8 ounces orecchiette into the boiling water and cook for 2 minutes. Remove with a spider or slotted spoon and add the pasta to the sausage pan with a spoonful or 2 of the pasta cooking water.

5. Turn the heat up to medium and toss or stir.

6. Add the broccoli rabe, continuing to toss or stir for about 2 minutes to continue cooking the pasta.

7. Add the chickpeas and butter and toss for 30 seconds.

8. Divide between two bowls and garnish with the pecorino sardo. Mangia bene, Vive felice!

> **Jenny** What's your favorite kind of pasta, Billy?
>
> **Billy:** Do I have to choose? But any pasta that the Queen of Pasta makes is going to for sure be my favorite.

CASSIE PIUMA

When we get calls or emails from friends visiting Boston asking us where the area's most unique place to eat is, 100 percent of the time we say Sarma in Somerville. One of us is more inclined to eat food he's used to, while the other looks for cuisine she's never tasted before. Both of us, however, are blown away whenever we taste seven-time James Beard–nominated chef/owner Cassie Piuma's envelope-pushing flavor combinations present on every small plate at Sarma.

Sarma means "to wrap" or "to envelop" like Chef Piuma's Cabbage Dolmades, but as we've gotten to know her, we also understand that her guests will also be wrapped in love and be treated to food and hospitality that comes from the heart. Since the restaurant opened in

2013, it's been a favorite of locals (and a place Jenny goes to for many occasions). Chef Piuma and her business partner and mentor Ana Sortun are responsible for putting Somerville on the culinary map with their Eastern Mediterranean meze dishes like Lamb Kofte Sliders and Garlic Shrimp Lamejun.

Chef Piuma grew up in Duxbury, Massachusetts, and as a girl would watch Mary Ann Esposito on TV hosting *Ciao Italia* and jot down recipes in a notebook. Chef Piuma is half Greek, and feta cheese was a staple in her diet, but she wasn't exposed to the flavors she would one day master. She'd planned on going to the University of Vermont to study medicine, but she trusted her gut and went to Johnson & Wales

University instead, where she got her degree in culinary arts. We're glad she made this choice, not only for the foodies but because this is where she met her husband Matthew Piuma, who would become general manager and co-owner of Sarma.

Chef Piuma gained invaluable experience by working at Al Forno in Rhode Island under the late George German. She then moved to Boston to work at Sel de la Terre and later as a sausage maker at the South End's The Butcher Shop. But it was when she worked at Oleana in Cambridge that she found the cuisine that ignited her imagination as well as recognition from tastemakers.

Chef Piuma told us that Oleana's Chef Sortun taught her about how to respect the rules before breaking them. She admires her mentor for being a pioneer who deeply cares about the impact her food makes on the community, and her thoughtful, honest presence has always provided inspiration and forward momentum. They travel to Turkey and the neighboring region often, and have paid homage to the spices and flavors from there that have captivated guests at their restaurants.

In their beautiful partnership, we see a lot of Ana in Cassie and a lot of Cassie in Ana.

Sarma is a relaxed gathering place based on the *meyhanes* of Turkey. You might find a musician playing an oud while guests devour combinations of the familiar and the extraordinary. Beet Kibbeh, Lentil Nachos, and Harissa BBQ Duck are just some of the locally sourced and flavorful options on Chef Piuma's menu. When she's not with her two daughters or running the restaurant, she finds time to give back with organizations like the Women's Lunch Place and by hosting toy drives for the children of Somerville.

STEAK GYROS WITH BLACK TRUFFLE TZATZIKI

Serves 4

This Greek sandwich uses steak instead of lamb, and seasoning as Chef Piuma has laid it out is a must for the best flavor. The tzatziki sauce is made bold with the addition of truffle.

To make the spice mix
1. Mix all ingredients in a bowl and set aside.

To make the basil toum
1. Place ingredients in a blender and puree to a smooth paste.

To make the black truffle tzaztiki
1. Grate cucumbers on the large holes of a box grater, then squeeze as much liquid out of them as possible. Discard liquid. This will keep your tzatziki thick.
2. Add grated cucumbers to a bowl with other ingredients and mix well.

To prepare the steak gyros
1. Brush each slice of beef with basil toum. Season liberally with spice mix and salt to taste.
2. Roll the beef up on itself from top to bottom, into a loose cylinder. Cut in half. You should have two separate rolls.
3. Thread rolls on skewers and drizzle with olive oil.
4. Grill on a hot surface for 2 to 3 minutes on each side.
5. Serve grilled skewers with tzatziki and a seasonal chopped salad, if desired.

CHEF'S TIP: If using wooden skewers for this recipe, soak them in water for at least 1 hour before grilling to keep them from burning.

For the spice mix
- 2 tablespoons dried oregano
- 1 tablespoon cumin
- 1 tablespoon ground coriander
- 1 teaspoon tarragon
- 1 teaspoon dried ground rosemary
- 1 teaspoon garlic powder
- 1 teaspoon paprika
- 1 teaspoon smoked paprika
- 1 teaspoon black pepper
- 1/4 teaspoon cinnamon

For the basil toum
- 1 small bunch basil
- 8 cloves garlic
- Juice and zest of 1 lemon
- 1 tablespoon red wine vinegar
- 1/2 cup canola oil
- Salt, to taste
- 1/2 cup olive oil

For the tzaztiki
- 4 Persian cucumbers
- 2 cups full-fat Greek yogurt
- 2 tablespoons olive oil
- 1 tablespoon truffle oil or shavings
- 1 tablespoon lemon juice
- 1 tablespoon finely minced garlic
- 1 teaspoon dried mint
- 1/2 bunch dill, finely chopped

For the steak
- 2½ pounds sirloin trimmed, sliced 1/4-inch lengthwise
- Salt, to taste
- Olive oil for drizzling

STEVE DIFILLIPPO AND RODNEY MURILLO

Before either of us hosted a TV show, we both knew master networker and Massachusetts Restaurant Hall of Famer Steve DiFillippo. Billy met what would become one of his great friends through Steve's father, the president of a company called Unifirst, who asked Billy to host company events. Steve's brother was also Billy's neighbor in Lynnfield, and their kids grew up together. Jenny, who was excited and nervous on her first day of production on *TV Diner*, was relieved that Steve, a giant in the industry, was their first guest. She knew him as an excellent father to her brother's best friend. One of the godfathers of hospitality in the city that has his heart, the chef and CEO of the Davio's Northern Italian Kitchen empire has deep and trusted connections not just with us but throughout the city and the country.

Steve combined his father's business acumen with his mother and grandmother's talent for cooking by earning a degree in marketing from Boston University as well as graduating from the Cambridge School of Culinary Arts. His first job in the restaurant business was as a dishwasher. At age twenty-four, he bought an established restaurant called Davio's, and over the years, turned it into a national brand with eleven restaurants.

Davio's always hosts a who's who of guests with the likes of Bruce Springsteen and Robert Kraft having dined there. But no matter who is eating at Davio's, Steve makes sure everyone is comfortable and taken care of. This doesn't just apply to guests. In almost forty years of being a part of this industry, Steve has made sure to treat his employees right. This has built a loyalty and affection for Steve among his staff.

One of the most special relationships is that between Steve and culinary director and vice president of Davio's, Chef Rodney Murillo.

Chef Murillo grew up in Costa Rica and came to Boston at age sixteen. He worked his way up the Davio's kitchen and has been with the company for decades. The two travel together to all of the Davio's restaurants and collaborate on the menus. But they're also great friends outside of work who will often spend holidays like the Fourth of July together, cooking for their families at Steve's house. They also spend their time giving back to organizations like Best Buddies, where Davio's employs workers from the Best Buddies Jobs program. It's a beautiful relationship that we've seen grow and evolve in an industry where collaborations don't always last.

With their Boston locations in Back Bay and the Seaport, Davio's consistently wows with their center cut of filet mignon or a strip steak aged for fifty-five days. But what makes Davio's a special steakhouse is the wide offering of Italian dishes, pastas, seafood, salads, and a brunch menu that we'll always wake up early for.

Steve DiFillippo is counted on by many, including former Governor Baker who appointed him to the Reopening Advisory Board to help restaurants get back to what they loved to do during the pandemic. He's been trusted to be the chef representing the New England Patriots at the Super Bowl's Party with a Purpose event. He's on the board of several non-profits, including The Greater Boston Food Bank, and *Boston* magazine has named him one of the Most Influential Bostonians for several years. To us, he's been a dear friend who finds time to check in even when he doesn't have time, and for that, we are forever grateful.

Steve has been a mentor to Jenny. When she was launching her sparkling wine, Champy, he gave invaluable advice on what to do and how. In Steve's bestselling book, *It's All About the Guest*, Billy was touched to find that Steve mentioned him as an inspiration in the culinary world. It's only right to put Steve DiFillippo in *our* book, because he's one of the best friends the city of Boston could have.

KOBE MEATBALLS

Makes about 24

These are not your average meatballs because Kobe beef is so tender. The texture is superb.

1. In a large bowl, mix breadcrumbs and milk and set aside.
2. Over medium-high heat, sauté onions and garlic with olive oil until soft (about 10 minutes). Transfer to a large bowl and let cool.
3. Add beef, veal, pork, both cheeses, herbs, eggs, and one teaspoon each of salt and pepper to the cooled onions; mix well.
4. Cover bowl with plastic wrap and refrigerate 1 hour or up to overnight.
5. Preheat oven to 350°F.
6. Remove meatballs from refrigerator and form into 3-ounce balls, about 2 inches, placing them on a cookie sheet as you make them.
7. On medium heat, heat 3 tablespoons vegetable oil in a large sauté pan, add meatballs without crowding the pan, and cook until brown on the outside (slightly pink on the inside) about 10 minutes.
8. Transfer cooked meatballs into large roasting pan or two 9- x 13-inch pans.
9. Repeat with remaining meatballs, adding more oil as needed.
10. Add tomato sauce to the roasting pan(s), making sure you have plenty of sauce (should be at least 1 inch over the top of the meatballs).
11. Cover with aluminum foil and bake for 1 hour.

- 3 cups breadcrumbs
- 1 cup whole milk
- 1 white medium onion, diced
- 1 clove garlic, minced
- 1/4 cup olive oil
- 1 pound ground American-style Kobe beef
- 1 pound ground veal
- 1 pound ground pork
- 1/2 cup grated parmesan
- 1/2 cup grated Romano cheese
- 1/4 cup chopped parsley
- 1/4 cup chopped basil
- 3 whole eggs, lightly beaten with a fork
- Salt and pepper, to taste
- Vegetable oil for frying
- 8 cups tomato sauce

Side Dish

THE GREATER BOSTON FOOD BANK

We take the responsibility of having a large audience seriously, not just because they trust us to tell them where they should visit, but because they also trust us to let them know where they can give back. From the outset, we have prioritized amplifying and championing non-profits in the food sector. Among these, The Greater Boston Food Bank stands out as a cornerstone, tirelessly providing nutritious meals to thousands across eastern Massachusetts through its extensive network of six hundred food pantries spanning 190 towns and cities. The work they do is crucial and unwavering, and the need for their efforts is at a staggering high.

The aftereffects of COVID-19 are still being felt, with one in three individuals in Massachusetts experiencing food insecurity. President and CEO Catherine D'Amato is extraordinary in leading the charge against hunger and has been working tirelessly with the organization since 1995. Witnessing her dynamic dedication firsthand, we've seen her drive and passion translate into nearly ninety million healthy meals being distributed annually.

These meals would not be possible without volunteers, donations, partnerships with businesses, and contributions from the hospitality industry. We've been honored to emcee events like their annual Chain of Giving fundraiser to keep the conversation about eradicating hunger present in people's minds and hearts, and we are proud to be in the company of chefs and restaurateurs who also make their support of The Greater Boston Food Bank a top priority.

Photo courtesy of The Greater Boston Food Bank

A Taste of Boston

TATIANA ROSANA

Tatiana Rosana is not only the executive chef of the Seaport's Envoy Hotel, but she's also a children's book author. Her picture book, *Arlo and the Secret Ingredient*, includes recipes that families can make together. Jenny's daughters, Vienna and Lenox, are big fans of this book, and we know those of you with little ones will be too.

Not to spoil the story too much, but what Arlo learns is that one of the most special ingredients you can add to any recipe is the most important thing of all: love. We've come to learn that this is an ingredient that Chef Rosana puts into everything she does.

She says her grandparents inspired her great work in the kitchen. Growing up in a Cuban household in Miami, Rosana learned from her grandmother how cooking and food can bring family and friends together. Her grandfather showed her the power of open-fire cooking and respecting ingredients. It makes sense that Chef Rosana opened Para Maria, a Latin-inspired restaurant dedicated to her grandmother Maria, in the Envoy to great success.

The Envoy's Lookout Rooftop and Bar is one of the hottest places in the city, especially in the summertime. Sure, the view is a big draw, but what keeps people coming back are the bar bites, brunch, and inventive cocktails like the Call Your Mom, a gin, tangerine, prosecco, and ginger concoction with a sugar rim.

Chef Rosana incorporates many different culinary influences from her life into her menus: French from her training at Le Cordon Bleu, Korean fare inspired by her wife's heritage, Cuban flavors from family in Florida, and New England classics from earlier in her career working at Harvest with Chef Mary Dumont and at the Mandarin Oriental Hotel with Chef Rachel Klein.

You may have seen Chef Rosana on your TV screen and not just on our show. (Though we hope we're her favorite hosts.) She's a *Chopped* champion, had opportunities to *Beat Bobby Flay*, is a supportive expert on *Bar Rescue*, and has appeared on many morning shows, showcasing her skills as anchors drool, waiting to dig into her creations. We have a feeling that Chef Rosana would argue that the real star of her household is her son, the real-life Arlo, who you can find on her Instagram, cooking with his moms. It looks like the whole family has plenty of the special ingredient at the ready.

The delicious Mojo Pork Taco is a secret family recipe, and trust us, we have asked what is in it, but we know only Tatiana can do her family's recipe just right. Lucky for us, she contributed a recipe for Paella de Mariscos, a seafood paella that you can make and put your own love into.

PAELLA DE MARISCOS

Serves 6 to 8

Paella de Mariscos is a gorgeous bouquet of seafood gently tucked into seasoned rice. Perfect for a party or special family meal.

1. In a large sauté pan, heat olive oil over medium-high heat.
2. Add chorizo and sauté for 3 minutes.
3. Add garlic, onion, and peppers and cook until translucent and fragrant (about 4 minutes).
4. Add paprika, oregano, and cayenne and lightly toast for 2 minutes. Add diced tomatoes and cook for another 2 minutes.
5. Add rice and stir until thoroughly coated and very lightly toasted. Deglaze with white wine and reduce by half.
6. Add chicken stock, saffron, and bay leaf and stir. Bring to a boil then reduce heat to a simmer.
7. Cook over medium-low heat for 15 minutes, then gently tuck shrimp, calamari, and mussels into rice. Top with peas and season with salt and pepper (be sure not to stir rice while cooking so you can achieve the crispy rice on the bottom of the pan). Cook another 5 to 10 minutes or until rice is tender and seafood is fully cooked.
8. Turn heat up to medium high and allow rice to toast on the bottom of the pan for 2 minutes. (Remember, no stirring.)
9. Remove pan from heat and garnish with lemon and parsley.

- 2 tablespoons olive oil
- 8 ounces dried chorizo sausage, small diced
- 3 cloves garlic, minced
- 1 Spanish onion, small diced
- 1 red bell pepper, small diced
- 1 tablespoon smoked paprika
- 1 tablespoon oregano
- 1/2 teaspoon cayenne
- 1 (14½-ounce) can diced tomatoes
- 2 cups short-grain rice (Chef Rosana prefers bomba)
- 1/2 cup white wine
- 4 cups chicken stock
- 1 pinch of saffron
- 1 bay leaf
- 10 jumbo shrimp (peeled and deveined)
- 8 ounces calamari rings
- 10 mussels
- 1/2 cup frozen peas
- Salt and pepper, to taste
- 1 lemon, cut into wedges
- 2 tablespoons parsley, minced

NIA GRACE

Have you ever watched an old Hollywood movie where the characters go to a supper club? It's always a cinematic, perfect place where everyone is dressed to the nines, the food is exquisite, there's a band, and a dance floor where guests get loose.

Those places seem to be extinct in real life, but there's one in Boston, thanks to Nia Grace. Grace by Nia, in the Seaport, is the brainchild of the local restaurateur and a partnership with the nightlife gurus Ed and Joe Kane and Randy Greenstein at Big Night Entertainment, known for enduring hotspots such as Empire, Big Night Live, and The Grand.

At Grace by Nia, guests are transported to another time but have access to a menu that represents the best of Boston kitchens.

It seems unfair to lead with décor because Grace's food is so good, but we have to talk about how special this place looks and feels. Guests head to the top floor of the Seaport building that houses the restaurant. They might pass a step and repeat backdrop for photos, which implies they're in the place to be seen.

Then the door opens, and it's glitz and glamor with the privacy of a speakeasy and the mood of that old movie supper club. There's live jazz and international music stars performing five nights a week, and it's warm; people seem ready to mingle, like troubles have been left behind.

And then there's the food. Grace has been working for years to get to this unforgettable menu. Creole Pasta, Curry Coconut Melange, Bourbon Peach Spare Ribs, and Lobster Mac and Cheese are just a few of the tempting dishes that accompany the live music.

Born and raised in Roxbury, Massachusetts, Nia went to the University of Miami and earned a degree in criminology, thinking that helping people through the law would be her calling. Later, she found a job at Darryl's Corner Bar & Kitchen in the South End, where she saw a restaurant find success with Southern food, live music, and a welcoming vibe to all. She was impressed with the vision of owner Darryl Settles and paid attention. She eventually bought the place—and has plans for it.

Another Grace by Nia will soon be opening at Foxwoods Casino in Connecticut. The woman with her name on the sign has been busy! The last time we shot a segment with Nia, she was about to get married and had worked twenty-nine days straight, not even taking a half day off for a whole month before her wedding. As tired as we thought she might be, she commanded an audience, greeted everyone with a smile and kind word, and even let Billy play on a drum on her stage.

Outside of her restaurants, Nia also helps build community by serving on the Massachusetts Restaurant Association's board of directors, and in 2020 she co-founded the Boston Black Hospitality Coalition, an organization designed to preserve and bolster Black-owned restaurants and businesses and foster the creation of new ones. Grace by Nia is the Boston Seaport's first Black-woman-owned and first Black-owned supper club to have a liquor license in Boston.

When Billy played a drum onstage at Grace by Nia, there wasn't an audience as large as the one superstar 50 Cent had when he started an impromptu sing-along onstage of "In Da Club" after enjoying his birthday dinner at Grace by Nia. If 50 Cent needs a drummer, Billy is available!

HOT MARYLAND CRAB DIP

Serves 10 to 12

Rich, creamy, with a hint of tang and plenty of Old Bay give this dip the Maryland touch—an appetizer great for entertaining family and friends.

1. Preheat oven to 375°F.
2. In large mixing bowl, combine cream cheese, mayonnaise, sour cream, lemon juice, and Worcestershire sauce and whisk until smooth.
3. Mix in Old Bay Seasoning.
4. Fold in 2 cups shredded cheddar jack and all the parmesan cheese.
5. Fold in crab meat and jalapeños.
6. Transfer to baking pan, porcelain casserole dish, or cast-iron skillet and top with remaining 1/2 cup shredded cheddar jack.
7. Bake at 375°F for 20 minutes or until brown and bubbling.

- 4 8-ounce bars cream cheese, softened
- 1/2 cup mayonnaise
- 2 cups sour cream
- 4 tablespoons lemon juice
- 2 tablespoons Worcestershire sauce
- 2 tablespoons Old Bay Seasoning
- 2½ cups shredded cheddar jack cheese, divided
- 2 cups shredded parmesan cheese
- 2 pounds lump crab meat, drained
- 2 fresh jalapeños, diced

JESUS PRECIADO

The Mediterranean is vast and encompasses a lot of flavors. It's been our impression that the Mazi Food Group is trying to explore *all* aspects of Mediterranean cuisine in their three South End restaurants: Kava Neo Taverna, Ilona, and Gigi. It's hard to master *one* type of cuisine, but chef and part-owner Jesus Preciado has been able to do it all. From Greek to Italian to Turkish to Georgian (the country, not the state) and so many culturally authentic dishes in between, Chef Preciado is busy overseeing all of the menus. But he's always easy to talk to and connect with and strikes us as having a great sense of balance.

Chef Preciado grew up in a small town in Colombia, and he never cooked. He studied electrical engineering at university, and at age twenty wanting to see the world and visit friends, came to Boston. After two weeks, he'd run out of money, and a friend said the restaurant he worked at, John Harvard's, needed a dishwasher. That was more than two decades ago, and Chef Preciado has worked his way up to become one of the most exciting chefs in the city.

Mazi means "together" in Greek. The Mazi Food Group, co-owned by Irakli Gogitidze and George Axiotis, has been able to bring people together to their exquisitely decorated and vibrant restaurants in a neighborhood they love and feel is very unique. Another way to bring people together? Chef Preciado's food!

At Kava Neo Taverna, it's strictly Greek from the menu to the wine and cocktails. There are small plates like Loukaniko Grilled Sausage or Kolokithakia Zucchini Chips with Tzatziki and entrees like Moussaka and Lavraki Mediterranean Sea Bass. Chef Preciado said he knew he was on the right track when a guest, an elderly Greek woman, came to visit him in the kitchen. She hugged him and in broken English said he'd done a good job.

Ilona, a lively and plush lounge and cocktail bar, offers a wider range of Mediterranean meze plates, including Shish Barak, pasta filled with onion, lamb, pinenuts, and yogurt sauce; Pikilia, a variety of brightly colored and flavorful dips; and Imeruli Khachapuri, a traditional Georgian bread filled with cheese, to name a few.

Gigi is all Italian, all the way. The space is modern yet vintage, and it feels like walking into a chic house party at an Italian villa of yesteryear. The pasta is homemade, their most popular cocktail is the Sophia Loren (citrus vodka, strawberry puree, lime juice, basil), and Chef Preciado's Arancini and Risotto al Manzo are not to be missed.

There's buzz about a new South End restaurant from the Mazi Food Group, Desnuda Cocina e Bar, opening soon. No matter what they plan on serving, we know Chef Preciado is up to the challenge.

UVETSI

Serves 4

This Greek stew is made with short ribs and orzo, an example of a Mediterranean dish that Chef Preciado has perfected over the years.

1. Salt the meat and rest it in the refrigerator for 8 to 12 hours.
2. Heat 3 tablespoons olive oil in a Dutch oven. Add onion and sauté for 15 to 20 minutes until nicely caramelized.
3. Add carrots and cook for another 5 minutes.
4. Add tomato paste and cinnamon stick.
5. Deglaze pan with red wine and reduce over medium-low heat until wine is evaporated, about 10 minutes.
6. Add the veal demi-glace, parsley, and chicken broth. Bring to a boil and let simmer while preparing the meat.
7. On a grill at high temperature or in a cast-iron pan on high, sear the meat on all sides, trying to use a minimum amount of oil.
8. Add the seared meat to the Dutch oven with the vegetables, mixing it in the sauce.
9. Cover and set in a 350°F oven for 2 hours and 20 minutes, until the meat is soft and juicy.
10. Precook the orzo for about 4 minutes in boiling water, strain, and add to the meat. Cook for another 20 minutes.
11. When ready, take it to the table!

12 ounces short ribs (about 5 pieces)
2 teaspoons salt
Olive oil for frying
4 cups chopped onion
3 cups chopped carrots
2 tablespoons tomato paste
1 large cinnamon stick
1 cup red wine
2 cups veal demi-glace
3/4 cup chopped parsley
1 quart chicken broth
1½ cup orzo

MICHAEL SERPA

There's heated debate about which lobster roll is better: the cold one with mayo or the warm one with butter? At Chef Michael Serpa's Little Whale Oyster Bar on Newbury Street, both are on the menu. But we've heard that those who can't decide are ordering the popular Lobster Spaghettini, topped with toasted garlic breadcrumbs, basil, and more than enough shaved parm to make people forget about mayo and butter altogether.

Serpa Hospitality specializes in seafood concepts made to stand out in a seafood-dense landscape. Select Oyster Bar in Back Bay, Atlántico in the South End, and Little Whale Oyster Bar all feature Chef Serpa's passion for adding flavors from his travels around the world to elevate New England staples.

Chef Serpa grew up in a family of Cuban chefs. His grandfather, father, and uncles on both sides of the family were all chefs in the restaurant business. His abuelas were amazing cooks who served up delicious Cuban classics. Chef Serpa spent his youth working summers in his father's Miami restaurant kitchen and his teen years working nights at local restaurants in Pennsylvania.

After graduating from The Culinary Institute of America, he found work in New York City at Olives under Chef Michael Crain. He came to Boston to work at Olives in Charlestown, then made his way to Neptune Oyster in the North End, which is where he met his wife Lina and made a name for himself as executive chef. Crowds lined up around the block to get in.

He ventured out on his own with Select Oyster Bar in 2015. The fifty-seat bistro in a Back Bay brownstone serves up the freshest catches with a unique flair. The Gloucester Swordfish is served with a pomegranate glaze and roasted eggplant puree, and the Maine Mussels are in a broth of toasted cashews, coconut milk, ginger, and aji Amarillo. It's no wonder *Boston* magazine named it Best Seafood Restaurant in 2019 and that Serpa Hospitality has continued to grow.

Atlántico, a bright and spacious tapas bar that pays tribute to Iberian, Spanish, and Portuguese cuisine, opened in the South End in 2020. The relaxed atmosphere is great for sharing Pulpo with Piquillo Peppers and White Asparagus Salad or Hamachi Crudo with friends, but for a large group, the Paella Atlántico overflowing with clams, mussels, prawns, squid, Maine lobster, and hake, is a sight to behold! Little Whale opened in 2022, and the cozy brownstone evokes memories of clam shacks from summers past but in a more refined setting.

We can tell when Chef Serpa is at one of his restaurants when his bicycle is parked outside. He not only bikes to his restaurants, but he's biked for the Pan Mass Challenge and for the Chefs Cycle for No Kid Hungry team. With his warm smile, he loves to tell the story behind each dish, about the person who caught the fish. His enthusiasm is infectious among his staff.

WHOLE ROASTED SEA BREAM "TAVERNA STYLE"

Serves 2

This is the first dish Chef Serpa had on the draft menu at Select. When he was opening the restaurant, he wanted to have a place to have very simply done seafood that showcased the quality of the product. Now you can try it too.

To make the salsa verde

1. Mix all ingredients together with just enough oil to make a paste. Set aside.

To make the vegetables

1. Roast fennel with the olive oil until tender, and showing a little color, and lightly brown.
2. Heat 2 tablespoons olive oil in a sauté pan. Add potatoes and sear until they have some color.
3. Add roasted fennel and salt, and pop into the oven with the fish toward the end of cooking.

To prepare the fish

1. Preheat oven to 500°F.
2. Pat dry and salt fish.
3. Heat canola oil in a large, seasoned cast-iron or griddle pan. Add fish and sear for approximately 90 seconds on each side.
4. Transfer to a sheet pan with some olive oil or butter on it.
5. Transfer to oven and bake for 8 to 10 minutes. You'll know the fish is cooked properly when the top fillet slides right off. When you pull the tail toward the head, the bottom fillet will be free. Clean up the smaller pin bones and enjoy.

To finish

1. When the fish is done and the thickest part next to the bones is cooked through and warm, remove and place on a bed of fennel and potatoes. Smother the fish with a big spoonful of the salsa verde. Garnish with lemon wedges.

For the salsa verde

- 1/2 cup chopped parsley
- 2 tablespoons chopped fresh oregano
- 2 tablespoons chopped fresh mint
- 3 tablespoons olive oil

For the vegetables

- 1 large fennel bulb, cleaned and roughly sliced
- 2 tablespoons olive oil
- 2 pounds fingerling potatoes, steamed and cut in half
- ½ teaspoon salt

For the fish

- 1 whole sea bream (dorade or branzino), scaled, gutted, and cleaned with ribs and spines removed
- Salt, to taste
- 1/4 cup canola oil
- 1 tablespoon olive oil or pad of butter for the pan

For the finish

- Lemon wedges

CHEF'S TIP: Make sure your purchased fish is gutted and scaled well. Using kitchen shears, snip the gills and smaller fins and cut a little notch near the tail to make filleting the fish easier.

THE NEBO SISTERS

We never laugh harder than when we're with Christine and Carla Pallotta, two of our favorite people on the planet whom we affectionately call the NEBO sisters.

They are the kindest and warmest people you'll ever meet; they make exquisite meals and are amazing storytellers.

We do warn our audiences that whenever the Pallotta sisters are around, there might be some colorful language. During one of their appearances on our show, Billy told viewers at home to ask their kids to leave the room. After a beat he felt safe asking Christine and Carla how they were doing and Christine responded, "F-ing great!"

Billy knew that one was coming and loved it.

Christine and Carla, who are chef/owners of Nebo Cucina and Enoteca, grew up in the North End in a loving Italian family where their mother and grandmother always had five meals cooking at the same time when preparing dinner for family and friends. When the sisters grew up, they had a successful spa and salon in Reading for twenty-seven years until they were ready for a change.

Christine told Carla she wanted to open a restaurant that would serve the kind of food their mother made for them, shareable family-style plates of delicious Italian food made from simple ingredients of the highest quality. And so, in 2005 they opened NEBO (which stands for North End Boston) in the North End.

Everything is made from scratch at NEBO, including their bestselling Zucchini Lasagna, which beat Bobby Flay's own recipe when the sisters appeared on *Throwdown with Bobby Flay*. Their handmade pastas like Strozzapreti Funghi and Spaghettini Alle Vongole are just like their mom made, and they can be confident about that. Why?

Mama Pallotta, now in her nineties, comes to the restaurant to do what the sisters call *quality control*. If Mama doesn't approve, it doesn't get served.

Mama Pallotta is not only beloved by her daughters, the rest of her family, and the NEBO staff, she's also adored by many of the 2008 championship Celtics players, who met her when she sat courtside. During Kevin Garnett's jersey retirement ceremony, he gave Mama Pallotta a big hug and smile. He'd been a fan of NEBO's arancini.

In 2013 the Pallotta sisters moved NEBO to the Atlantic Wharf, where their giant floor-to-ceiling windows give patrons a spectacular view of the Rose Kennedy Greenway. In summer on the patio outside, it's a little like you're out on a Boston-style piazza.

You'll fill up on cioppino with fresh New England seafood, the pizzas, or the spuckie sandwiches at lunch (the Milano with the crispy chicken milanese is not to be missed), but save some room for dessert. The spumoni sundae is our recommendation for a sweet ending.

POLENTA CON SCAMPI FRITTI

Serves 4

This Polenta con Scampi Fritti is Mama Pallotta–approved and sure to bring loved ones to the table every time. Quality control, however, is up to you at home.

To make the polenta

1. In a medium saucepan, bring water and salt to a boil.
2. Mix both types of cornmeal together, then slowly pour into boiling water, stirring continuously. Lower heat to medium.
3. Add 1 tablespoon olive oil. Stir until the mixture pulls away from the pan and is very thick, 15 to 20 minutes.
4. Butter a 9- x 9-inch pan. Spread polenta onto the pan evenly and let cool for 15 minutes. Cover with plastic wrap and refrigerate to set until ready to use.
5. When ready, cut polenta into 4-inch squares using a pastry cutter. Brush both sides with some of the olive oil.
6. In a frying pan, heat the rest of the olive oil. Place squares into pan and cook until polenta releases easily. Turn over and repeat.

To make the scampi fritti

1. Mix all dry ingredients together except seasoning salt.
2. In a bowl, soak shrimp in buttermilk for 1/2 hour.
3. In a large frying pan, heat olive oil.
4. Take a pinch of the dry mix and throw in the olive oil to see if it bubbles.
5. When bubbling, the oil is ready.
6. Dredge shrimp in dry mix and cook in olive oil. Preferably in 2 batches.
7. Place on paper towel and sprinkle with salt.

To make the scampi sauce

1. In a skillet over medium heat, melt butter with oil.
2. When butter starts to foam, add garlic.
3. Lower heat. Add shrimp shells.
4. Sauté until shells are no longer translucent.

For the polenta

4 cups water

1 teaspoon kosher salt

3/4 cup fine cornmeal

1/4 cup coarse cornmeal

1 tablespoon butter for pan

1/2 cup olive oil, divided

For the scampi fritti

20 large shrimp (peeled and deveined, saving shells for sauce)

1 cup buttermilk to soak

1/2 cup fine cornmeal

1/2 cup coarse cornmeal

1 teaspoon salt

1 cup of light extra-virgin olive oil

Extra salt for seasoning

For the scampi sauce

1 stick of unsalted butter

1/4 cup extra-virgin olive oil

2 garlic cloves, chopped fine

Shells from shrimp

2 tablespoons chopped parsley, divided

Juice of 1 lemon

5. Remove the shells and add 1 tablespoon parsley and lemon juice. Remove skillet from heat.

To assemble

1. Place one grilled polenta square on a dish.
2. Cover with 1/4 of the lemon butter sauce.
3. Place five shrimp around polenta.
4. Sprinkle with remaining chopped parsley.

> **Jenny:** I don't care who you are, you can't be around the Pallotta sisters and not laugh hysterically. They are so thoughtful, so warm, and I've never met funnier people.
>
> **Billy:** And their food is always (insert word I can't say on air but the sisters might here) amazing.

KWASI KWAA

One of the most special places in the city is an unassuming, welcoming spot in Upham's Corner in Dorchester. By day, it's a bright café where you can work or meet up with a friend while enjoying The Dreamer breakfast sandwich. By night, it's a full-service, thirty-seat dining room where reservations are hard to come by. *Very* hard to come by.

We're talking about Comfort Kitchen, a place where you'll not only enjoy a fantastic meal, but you'll learn the origins of the food you're eating and how food really brings all of us together.

In 2024, there weren't many big Boston names on the list of James Beard honorees. But Comfort Kitchen was the James Beard finalist for Best New Restaurant.

The *New York Times* named Comfort Kitchen one of The 50 Restaurants We're Most Excited About Right Now in 2023 and one of The 25 Best Restaurants in Boston in 2024.

That's no surprise to us. With dishes like Jerk Roasted Duck served with rice and peas; Za'tar Brown Butter Trout served with a smoked eggplant puree, tomato salad, and a green onion chimichurri sauce; and Jerk Jackfruit Sliders you won't believe are vegan, Comfort Kitchen is highlighting food from the African diaspora as well as dishes from along the spice trail. And it's all excellent.

Comfort Kitchen began when managing partner Biplaw Rai teamed up with chef partner Kwasi Kwaa after working together in the kitchens of Hi-Rise Bread Company in Cambridge and at Dudley Café in Roxbury. Both had immigrated to the US when they were young, Rai from Nepal and Kwaa from Ghana. They went on to spend years working in the Boston restaurant scene.

It wasn't lost on them how many restaurants and kitchens benefit from immigrant labor, nor that the efforts of those culinary workers weren't always in the spotlight. Rai and Kwaa wanted to own a restaurant where the food of immigrants—especially those who worked for them—would always be celebrated as the main event.

They started as a pop-up experience in Jamaica Plain, but everyone hoped they could turn the place into a brick-and-mortar restaurant. They wound up finding a comfort station—basically, a 1912 rest stop from the streetcar days—and, with help from Historic Boston Inc., they made the space their own. Rai and Kwaa co-own the restaurant with organization development partner Nyacko Pearl Perry and branding partner Rita Ferreira, who also happen to be their spouses, respectively.

On any day, there might be six languages spoken by the staff, a group who behaves more like a family when they have a meal together before dinner service. Go prepared to travel and learn. Every dinner menu has detailed information about the history of okra, plantains, curry chicken, and other ingredients.

Just make reservations early. It might be a few months before you get in.

JOLLOF RICE WITH GINGER RED WINE BRAISED GOAT

Makes 3 to 4 servings

Jollof Rice is a West African favorite and Ghanaian staple. The spices and scotch bonnets in the tomato base give it the kick we love. It's famous in West Africa for a reason . . . and famous for its debate on who makes it better! As a native of Ghana, Kwasi is definitely biased in that debate, but either way, the goal is to make it famous in Boston too!

The vibrant color comes from the tomato base, packed with spices, chilis, and ginger. Give it time to slowly simmer before adding in the rice, then let that do its thing and soak up all those great flavors.

To make the jollof rice

1. Sautée diced onions, garlic, chilis, and ginger in olive oil until caramelized, but not too browned. Add tomato paste and cook on medium heat, for about 5 minutes, letting the tomato bloom out (this cooks out the acidity).

2. Deglaze as needed with 1/4 cup water or vegetable stock (adding liquid to the hot pan is a process that helps break down the extra flavors and ingredients that tend to stick to the bottom of the pan as the acid in the tomato paste cooks out).

3. Add tomato puree and let all ingredients stew together for about 15 minutes (the flavor intensifies the longer it stews).

4. Taste and adjust seasoning as needed, then add basil and let simmer for a few minutes.

5. Remove basil, add rice, and stir to coat the rice with the paste that's developed. Add 1½ cup veg stock or water to submerge the rice.

6. Bring rice to just simmer, then drop heat to low and cover.

7. Check rice periodically, stirring to make sure it's cooking evenly. This process usually takes around 20 minutes, but it will depend on the rice and amount of heat. For best results, allow rice to steam until it sticks to the bottom of the pan. (Traditionally, jollof rice cooks like a paella and creates a crispy crust at the bottom that insulates the rice as it cooks and intensifies the flavors).

For the jollof rice

- 1 large yellow onion, diced
- 1 teaspoon minced garlic
- 1½ teaspoons minced scotch bonnet chilis (for less heat, can be substituted with habanero chilis)
- 1½-inch piece of ginger, minced or grated
- 2 tablespoons olive oil
- 1 teaspoon tomato paste
- 2 cups vegetable stock or water
- 4 large tomatoes, chopped
- 1 sprig of basil (leaves and stems)
- 2 cups rice (basmati or jasmine)

For the Ginger Red Wine Braised Goat

- 2 pounds goat meat, cut into 2½–3-ounce pieces
- 1 teaspoon curry powder
- Salt and black pepper, to taste
- 3 tablespoons olive oil
- 1 medium onion, large diced
- 1 medium carrot, large diced
- 2 pieces ginger, rough chopped
- 2 garlic cloves, smashed
- 1/2 cup red wine
- 1 tablespoon tomato paste

To make the Ginger Red Wine Braised Goat

1. Preheat oven to 325°F.
2. Season goat meat generously with the curry powder, salt, and pepper.
3. In a large oven-safe pot or Dutch oven, heat olive oil and brown the seasoned meat.
4. Remove meat from pot and set aside in a bowl.
5. Add onion, carrot, ginger, and garlic to the pot and lightly sauté until onions are soft and translucent.
6. Deglaze pot with red wine, scraping any brown bits, and let it reduce by half.
7. Add tomato paste and allow to bloom out.
8. Create an herb bundle by tying together the thyme, bay leaf, and parsley stems. This makes it easier to locate and remove at the end. Add bundle to the pot. Add scotch bonnet.
9. Return meat to the pot along with any accumulated juice, nestled as close together as possible.
10. Add stock until meat is just submerged, bring to a boil, cover, and braise in the oven for about 1½ hours or until tender.
11. After meat is cooked remove from the braise liquid. Remove bundle of herbs. Let sauce cool and skim fat from top, pulse liquid and veg together and serve sauce with goat.
12. Taste and adjust seasoning as needed. Serve with side of jollof rice.

6 sprigs of thyme

1 bay leaf

Small bunch of parsley stems (optional)

1 scotch bonnet pepper, cut in half

3 cups chicken stock

CHEF'S TIP: If goat is difficult to find, you can use lamb for this recipe as well.

JODY ADAMS

Restauranteur, chef, philanthropist, activist, and all-around creative thinker Jody Adams has said her success can be traced back to the influence and generosity of her friend, the late Julia Child. We're sure she learned plenty from the late, great culinary hero, but we also know that Adams is a star on her own—and has a special brand of hospitality that has set the tone for so many in the city.

Adams's restaurants have been destinations for decades. But her work behind the scenes has also shaped the look of who runs kitchens in our city. She's paved the way for other female (and really all) chefs who worked with her to flourish. She also fosters a culture of respect in an industry that can be challenging, overwhelming, and relentless. Over the years, we've heard from so many of Adams's staffers that she's taught them how to do incredible work without losing themselves in the hustle.

All of this makes sense to us. When Chef Adams was an undergrad studying anthropology at Brown University, she wanted a job where she could help people, and thought she'd be a nurse practitioner. It was when she volunteered as a dishwasher at a Planned Parenthood fundraiser that she met the keynote speaker, Chef Julia Child.

Years after Chef Adams had graduated and traveled abroad, she was managing a gourmet food store in Rhode Island. She wanted to work in restaurants, but it seemed a daunting industry to enter, especially as a woman in the 1980s. As luck would have it, Chef Adams was re-introduced to Julia Child when she walked into the store. Adams told Child that she hoped to work in the culinary business, and Child told her: Go work for Lydia Shire at Seasons in the Bostonian Hotel.

Chef Adams wound up working as a line cook for Lydia Shire's sous chef, Gordon Hamersley. When he started Hamersley's Bistro, he asked Chef Adams to join him as *his* sous chef. She learned about French technique and cuisine as one of the only chefs in the kitchen, as well as about how to run a restaurant.

She raised her Italian and New England culinary game by working as executive chef at Michela Larson's Michela's while raising two children with her husband, photographer Ken Rivard. (He's also the photographer and co-author of Chef Adams's cookbook!)

When Chef Adams opened Rialto with Chef Larson, the praise kept pouring in. For twenty-two years, Rialto, in Charles Hotel in Harvard Square, was where the who's who of Boston went to feast on gorgeous regional Italian creations. Chef Adams took over the restaurant on her own and wound up winning the James Beard Award for Best Chef: Northeast and mentoring chefs like Joanne Chang.

Now Chef Adams, in partnership with Eric Papachristos and Jon Mendez, is the co-owner of Trade in the Atlantic Wharf, Porto in the Prudential Center, Saloniki Greek with multiple locations in Boston and Cambridge, and the brand new La Padrona in the Raffles Boston Hotel. She has us covered from casual cuisine to a special night out with a loved one. It's her leadership in the kitchen that fosters a new generation of chefs to grow and pay their lessons forward to mentor others.

She's used her celebrity not only as a contestant on shows like *Top Chef Masters* but to bring attention and resources to Share Our Strength, The Greater Boston Food Bank, and Partners in Health, where she's a trustee and has traveled to helm culinary teams in Haiti and Rwanda. She co-founded Massachusetts Restaurants United and has biked for fourteen years in the Pan Mass Challenge with her team to help raise over a million dollars for cancer research. She is royalty to us, and we're sure Child would be proud.

RICOTTA GNOCCHI WITH MUSHROOMS

Serves 4 to 6

Elegant, rich, earthy, and balanced, this recipe will impress dinner guests time and again

To make the mushroom sauce

1. Put the mushrooms into a large sauté pan and cover with a lid. Cook over a medium heat until the mushrooms have given up their liquid, about 6 minutes.

2. Remove lid, season with salt and pepper, and cook until most of the liquid has evaporated.

3. Add butter, shallots, and garlic, and cook until they are tender and the mushrooms start to sear, about 5 minutes.

4. Add the Marsala and thyme, and cook until the Marsala has reduced by half.

5. Add cream to the mushrooms and Marsala to make a slightly soupy sauce. Taste and adjust the seasoning as necessary.

To make the ricotta gnocchi

1. In a stand mixer, whip together ricotta and eggs on the fastest setting until smooth, about 5 minutes.

2. Reduce speed and add lemon zest, all-purpose flour, and salt, mix for 2 minutes.

3. Put dumpling dough in a piping bag and refrigerate for 1/2 hour to chill.

4. On a flat, clean surface, spread a generous layer of semolina flour.

5. Cut the piping bag so the tip has a 1/2-inch wide hole.

6. Pipe a line of the ricotta dough, about 12 inches long, onto semolina.

7. Generously sprinkle semolina flour over the piped dough.

8. Using a paring knife, cut ricotta dough into 1-inch lengths.

9. Using a bench scraper, flip dumplings over, covering with semolina flour on all sides and transfer to a sheet pan dusted with semolina.

10. Continue until you've used up all the dough.

11. In a pot of boiling water seasoned with salt, cook dumplings for 3 minutes. Dumplings should have a creamy inside.

For the mushroom sauce

- 1½ pounds assorted mushrooms (oyster, shiitakes, chanterelles, cremini) cleaned and stems trimmed or removed
- Kosher salt and freshly ground black pepper
- 2 tablespoons unsalted butter
- 3 tablespoons minced shallot
- 2 teaspoons minced garlic
- 1/2 cup dry Marsala wine
- 1/2 teaspoon chopped fresh thyme
- 1 cup heavy cream

For the ricotta gnocchi

- 1 pound dry, high-quality ricotta (Chef Adams prefers Calabro), drained and strained for 30 minutes
- 2 eggs, beaten
- Zest and juice of 1 Meyer lemon
- 1 cup unbleached all-purpose flour
- 1 tablespoon kosher salt
- 2 cups semolina flour
- Unsalted butter
- 1/4 cup mixed chopped herbs (parsley, tarragon, basil)

(Continued)

12. Meanwhile, scoop a cup or so of pasta water into a large deep-sided sauté pan over medium heat.
13. Whisk in butter (remove chopped herbs) a few tablespoons at a time until emulsified and at a sauce consistency.
14. Stir in the chopped herbs, lemon juice, and freshly ground black pepper.
15. Toss the gnocchi in the butter.

To finish

1. Serve cooked gnocchi on mushroom sauce with a generous shaving of Parmesan cheese.
2. Garnish with chervil or parsley leaves.

Lemon juice from the Meyer lemon

Freshly ground black pepper, to taste

For the finish

Freshly grated Parmigiano Reggiano

Chervil or parsley leaves, for garnish

CHEF'S TIP: For this recipe, you want to keep small mushrooms intact and cut the bigger ones in half or quarters. You can leave them whole if they small enough or cut into 1½-inch pieces.

CHEF'S TIP: Make sure the ricotta is strained, once out of the strainer put the cheese on a double layer of paper towel to insure there is little moisture.

CHEF'S TIP: You can freeze the uncooked dumplings and store for later use.

DAVID DANIELS

As far as Billy is concerned, no one need wish him a happy birthday again after the astounding birthday bash Jenny and his wife Michele planned for him at the gorgeous Boston Harbor Hotel. It was a night done right with hospitality, stunning views of the water, and incredible food that we've come to expect from one of the premier hotels in the city.

We've featured the hotel on our show many times and became close with award-winning Chef Daniel Bruce. Chef Bruce, a consummate pro who helmed the kitchen at the hotel for thirty years, is the founder of the Boston Wine and Food Festival and was always a generous host to guests. To be the chef of a renowned five-star hotel with so many events is a huge responsibility and requires an immense amount of skill. When Chef Bruce retired, the hotel had almost impossible shoes to fill. Thankfully, the personable and talented Chef David Daniels is more than up to the challenge.

The Boston native is first-generation Italian and grew up watching his nonni and mother make everything from scratch using ingredients from the garden. At age eight, he knew he wanted to be a chef and practiced with recipes from a *Betty Crocker Cookbook for Kids* gifted to him from his nonni.

He first worked at the Boston Harbor Hotel in 1987 when he was twenty years old. Since his first time working at the hotel, he's gained *a lot* of experience. He was the executive chef at the OAK Long Bar

+ Kitchen at the Fairmont Copley Plaza and at Aragosta at the Fairmont Battery Wharf, and he was the culinary director for Sidell Hospitality and Bespoke Hospitality.

Chef Daniels also knows what to do when it comes to events. He's been a featured chef at the Nantucket Wine Festival and the Sundance Film Festival, to name a few, so he can handle all it takes to execute many of the Boston Harbor Hotel's happenings, including one of our favorites, the annual Summer in the City concert series.

It's now a full circle moment to be back at the hotel where he started his career. Everything on his menu at Rowes Wharf Sea Grille is like being presented with a piece of art and his flavors are exceptional. The Maine Diver Scallops served with a parsnip-truffle puree and the Ricotta Sugar Pumpkin ravioli are so good, the only thing that can enhance them is the amazing view of the harbor as the ships sail by.

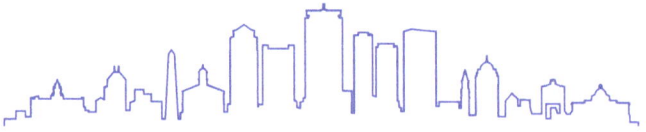

NANTUCKET BAY SCALLOPS IN THE STYLE OF OUR MEUNIÈRE

Serves 4

Nantucket Bay scallops are one of Nantucket's prized local bounties, enjoyed by hand harvesting and commercially fished alike.

To prepare the scallops

1. In a large skillet over medium heat, melt butter and sauté scallops on one side until golden brown.
2. Add bacon and cream, and bring to a boil. Cook until mixture coats scallops.
3. Add chives, lemon juice, parmesan cheese, and salt and pepper to taste.
4. Stir to combine.

To prepare the parmesan foam

Combine all ingredients and cook over medium heat. Add to bain-marie. Whisk with small hand blender until foamy.

To finish

Place each scallop in a small, individual scallop shell (or small dish) and top with parmesan cheese Foam.

For the scallops
- 2 tablespoons butter
- 20 bay or other small scallops, shells reserved
- 1/4 cup diced, rendered bacon, about 2 slices sauteed nice and crispy
- 1/2 cup heavy cream
- 1 tablespoon minced chives
- 1/2 teaspoon lemon juice
- 1/4 cup parmesan cheese, grated
- Salt and pepper, to taste

For the parmesan foam
- 1/2 cup whole milk
- 1 tablespoon butter
- 1 tablespoon parmesan cheese powder
- 1/2 cup chicken stock

For the finish
- Parmesan cheese

CHEF'S TIP: Heat parmesan foam to 125°F for ultimate effect.

HALEY FORTIER AND KATHRYN BRITTEN

After visits to some sleek and intimate wine bars in New York City (yeah, yeah, we guess *that* city has some cool things) sommelier and restaurateur Haley Fortier realized there weren't places like that in Boston proper. She also noticed that a lot of the wine lists weren't as inclusive or as special as she thought they could be. Lucky for us, she created and runs two wine bars, Downtown Crossing's haley.henry and Fenway's Nathálie.

Her wine lists are so rare and awesomely curated that *Food & Wine* magazine named her one of 2019's Sommeliers of the Year and the James Beard foundation has named haley.henry semi-finalist for Outstanding Wine Program in 2023, 2020, and 2019.

Cool, personable, confident, funny, and always happy to explain the difference between organic and biodynamic wine with guests, Fortier's commitment to educating wine enthusiasts and novices alike with small batch natural wines created by women, and bottles from wineries that don't always get the spotlight, has earned her a devoted following as well as national attention. She's a respected part of the Boston culinary scene and is always striving to learn more about wine, the people who make it, and making sure women, minority, and LGBTQ+ winemakers are celebrated.

The Woodshill, New Hampshire, native was a star soccer player in high school, worked as a sports photographer, and was even a corrections officer in the Boston city jail for six years. From there she went on to work as a server at Chart House, and four years later she was in charge of the restaurant's wine tastings. When she started working at Barbara Lynch's Sportello in 2008, she met wine director Cat Silirie, who gave wine classes every Tuesday and whose mentorship led Fortier on the path to creative thinking outside of the box.

Using her savings, and having the support of loyal Sportello customers who believed in Fortier's vision and invested in her, Fortier opened haley.henry in 2016. The charming hideaway bar is 680 square feet; big on personality, good vibes, and nibbles to enhance the wine selection.

Executive Chef Kathryn Britten, a Duxbury native who studied at the Culinary Institute of Charleston, South Carolina, and worked at many sushi restaurants in Charleston for fifteen years before returning to Massachusetts, is in charge of the eats at haley.henry.

The menu headings are odes to hip-hop, music that can often be heard at haley.henry and the larger sister wine bar that features even more woman-produced wine, Nathálie. The Biggie Small Plates at haley.henry feature dishes such as Deviled Eggs with Crispy Prosciutto and Chives, and Roasted Oysters in Herbed Garlic Butter. The All I Do Is Tin section is all about fish in tins, including Portugese Damorgada Tuna Belly in Olive Oil. Selections from the Bone Thugs & Charcuterie section include boards with Duck Rillette, Chicken Liver Mousse, and cheeses from Spain, France, and the Netherlands. But Chef Britten really shines with dishes like Red Snapper Ceviche, Sesame-Crusted Tuna served with a Carrot Ginger Puree, and her Creamsicle Panna Cotta for a sweet ending.

DUCK RILLETTE

Serves 4 to 6

This recipe is one of the classics at haley.henry. It's great as a snack anytime, but can easily be served for dinner with toast points and a simple salad.

To make the duck confit

1. Season duck legs with salt. Place in a large container or zipper lock bag along with the thyme, garlic, and black peppercorns. Cover the container or seal the bag and refrigerate overnight or up to 24 hours.

2. The following day, rinse duck legs with cold water and pat dry.

3. Preheat oven to 300°F.

4. Place duck legs in a baking dish large enough for them to fit snugly in a single layer.

5. Heat duck fat in a saucepan just enough to turn the fat to liquid. Pour duck fat over the duck legs to cover completely, then pour an extra 1/2 inch or so of the duck fat over the legs to ensure they stay completely submerged during cooking.

6. Cover baking dish with tin foil and place on a sheet tray in case there is any spillover during cooking.

7. Cook for 4 hours, then remove from oven. Keep duck legs in the cooking fat and let cool to room temperature. Once at room temperature, keep in the fridge, covered in the fat until you are ready to use.

To make the duck rillette

1. Heat duck legs in duck fat just enough to liquify the fat. Pull duck legs out and reserve fat for future use. Shred meat and skin from duck legs, making sure to remove any bones or gelatinous bits.

2. Place shredded duck into a mixer fitted with a paddle attachment. Add remaining ingredients and mix well. Taste for seasoning and add more salt and duck fat if needed.

3. Transfer mixture into glass jars. Cover with a layer of duck fat to preserve for future use or serve immediately. Keep in the refrigerator for up to 2 weeks.

For the duck confit

- 6 duck legs
- 1 tablespoon kosher salt
- 6 sprigs thyme
- 6 garlic cloves, smashed
- 1 tablespoon whole black peppercorn
- 1½ pounds duck fat

For the duck rillette

- 2 tablespoons duck fat
- 1/4 cup chives
- 1 shallot, finely diced
- Zest and juice from 3 oranges
- 2 tablespoons Angostura bitters
- Kosher salt, to taste

CHEF'S TIP: This duck confit recipe is the basis for our Duck Rillette, but you can use these for a variety of dishes. We love to place the confit legs in the broiler to create a simple crispy duck leg.

CHEF'S TIP: Confit duck legs can be homemade, or you can purchase them in specialty grocery stores or online.

TONY SUSI

Bar Enza in Harvard Square's Charles Hotel states that it has the best Italian cuisine in Cambridge. With Executive Chef Tony Susi in the kitchen, a veteran chef who was born and raised in the North End to an Italian family, lives in the North End, has traveled to Italy, and has spent decades specializing in Italian food among other cuisines in prestigious restaurants, they're a thousand percent right.

Bar Enza, a neo-modern trattoria, is a part of the Lyons Group, which excels at bringing fun and exceptional dining and entertainment concepts to the city. Patrick Lyons, the owner of the Lyons Group, has had an enormous impact on the city and is a leader who for decades has had his finger on the pulse of where people want to go at night. The group behind Scampo, Sonsie, Kings Dining and Entertainment, Summer Shack, and many other of our favorite places to eat and play opened Bar Enza in 2021 where famed Rialto and Benedetto used to be.

Chef Susi's career started when he was a teen working in the kitchens of North End restaurants Mamma Maria's and Davide. His parents hailed from Sulmona in the Abruzzi region of Italy, and he traveled there, soaking up the culture that helps inform his culinary prowess.

He had decades of experience at restaurants like Olives in Boston and in New York. His cooking has been lauded by the *Boston Globe*, the *New York Times*, and *Food & Wine* magazine to name a few.

Now at Bar Enza, with a menu that changes with the seasons, Chef Susi takes Italian classics and puts his own current spin on them. As one of the best pasta makers in the city, he has revamped the menu to play up to his strengths of making dishes approachable yet unique. The Fazzoletti, Chef Susi's version of a handkerchief lasagna, is filled with spinach and fontina cheese and baked with bechamel before being topped with fresh tomatoes, and is just a fraction of the goodness he's cooking up.

We meet with clients and business partners at Bar Enza, and Chef Susi always goes out of his way to give us a memorable experience. He's able to connect with people not only through his food but with his generosity of spirit.

SQUASH TORTELLI, BROWN BUTTER, TOASTED ALMONDS, PECORINO ROMANO FONDUTA

Serves 4

Fonduta is the Italian version of fondue. Chef Susi recommends being generous with the fonduta for this decadent dish.

To make the pecorino Romano fonduta

1. Start by simmering the water and corn starch, bring to a quick boil.

2. Whisk in the olive oil and then the cheese, stirring constantly until thick and smooth. Transfer to a blender and spin 3 to 4 minutes.

3. Season with salt and pepper as needed, cover, and set aside in a warm area of the stove top.

To make the pasta

1. Add water and salt to a pot large enough to accommodate the pasta and bring to a boil.

2. Place a large sauté pan on low heat; add the cubed butter, rosemary, and a generous pinch of salt; continue to simmer and brown the butter.

3. In the meantime, place the pasta in boiling water, cook until the center is tender. By this time the butter should be brown. Gently ladle in some pasta water to stop the browning and emulsify the butter sauce.

4. Using a hand strainer, remove the pasta from the water directly into the sauté pan. Gently stir the pasta with the butter sauce using additional pasta water if needed.

5. Add the grated Romano cheese, taste for seasoning, and begin to spoon out on serving plates.

For the finish

1. Generously spoon fonduta over the pasta.

2. Sprinkle with toasted almonds and serve.

For the pecorino Romano fonduta

2 cups water

3 tablespoons corn starch

1/4 cup extra-virgin olive oil

4 cups grated Romano cheese

Kosher salt, to taste

Coarse black pepper, to taste

For the pasta

8 tablespoons butter, cubed

1 sprig rosemary, removed from stem

Kosher salt

2 dozen squash-filled tortelli or ravioli

1/2 cup grated pecorino Romano

For the finish

1 cup sliced almonds, toasted

BRIAN MOY

Boston's Chinatown is one of the oldest Chinatowns in the country, and it's where restaurateur and owner of the Shōjō Group, Brian Moy, grew up. Seeing how the neighborhood has changed with more young professionals moving in nearby high-rises, but wanting to preserve the heart and soul of the neighborhood he loved so much, Chef Moy has created fun pan-Asian locales that make the traditional fresh and the fresh traditional.

Restaurants like Shōjō in Chinatown, Cambridge, and Logan Airport; Ruckus noodle bar in Chinatown; China Pearl in Quincy; and Nomai (the more sophisticated older sibling to Shōjō) in Hingham, have wowed us and the Boston crowd with food that's designed to bring people from all neighborhoods to the table.

Brian was raised in the hospitality industry, working in his family's restaurants, like the dim sum institution China Pearl in Chinatown, since he was a kid in the 1980s. He bussed tables, worked as a waiter and floor manager, and learned how to speak to guests and build community from the neighboring street vendors who sold fruit. He watched Martin Yan's *Yan Can Cook* and Ming Tsai's *East Meets West* on TV, seeing how Chinese food was being highlighted and embraced in the mainstream media.

His father, Ricky Moy, whom he saw work tirelessly in the kitchen and front of house, encouraged Brian to get in any other line of work than restaurants. Brian did graduate from Boston University, but he couldn't shake the passion for the world he'd grown up in. When he read in David Chang's *Momofuku* cookbook that Chang put foods he enjoyed eating himself on the menu, Brian realized if his restaurants were going to be successful, he had to create a menu and ambience that *he* enjoyed and knew others would too.

Shōjō opened next door to China Pearl in 2012 and is one of the funkiest and coolest places in the whole city. With hip-hop blasting; colorful graffiti mural art adorning the walls; an extensive Japanese whiskey list; and menu items like the Shōjōnator, a beefy burger served in a house-made bao bun with Sriacha aioli, smoked BBQ sauce, bacon, KimCheese, and fried shallots, the happening restaurant brings in lots of young folks (and the young at heart)!

Shōjō continues to be a gastropub and cocktail bar that always feels like a party. Whether you're there for brunch to enjoy the Coconut 5 Spice French Toast, or if the Bruins game went into overtime and you need a late-night bite, indulge in the Duck Fat Fries, a Chopped Cheese Bao, or Wu-Tang Tiger Style Ribs slathered in a hoisin and Thai barbecue sauce.

Brian knows his father is proud of the Shōjō Group restaurants. We have a feeling he's also proud of Brian's commitment to excellent hospitality, food, his family, his support of the Joslin Diabetes Center's Asian American Diabetes Initiative, and his community in Chinatown and beyond.

BÒ LÚC LẮC (VIETNAMESE SHAKING BEEF)

Serves 4

This is a recipe I cook at home a lot and also serve it at Shōjō Cambridge, where we have our original Shōjō classic favorites along with fun, elevated Southeast Asian dishes with our Shōjō twist!

To make the pickled red onions

1. Place sliced red onion into a jar, cup, or large bowl.

2. Combine vinegar, water, sugar, salt in a pot and bring to a boil. Stir to dissolve all ingredients and let cool down to warm.

3. Pour marinade over sliced onions and let sit for 1 hour or until onions turn pink in color.

4. Remove onions from the pickling juice and set aside.

To prepare the steak

1. Place steak cubes into mixing bowl with garlic, fish sauce, soy sauce, oyster sauce, and brown sugar. Mix to combine. Add cracked pepper to your liking and mix well. Let rest for at least 30 minutes to marinate.

2. Heat large pan with some oil on medium heat. Add red onions and let them cook for 2 minutes. Add marinated steak and cook for 1 to 2 minutes on each side to brown. This will cook the steak to medium temperature, cook longer for more well done if you like.

To finish

1. Place watercress on a large plate, with sliced tomatoes on top.

2. Once steak is cooked, place directly onto the watercress and tomato on the plate. If multiple rounds of steak will be cooked, place directly on top of the watercress and tomato each round when finished.

3. Pouring remaining juices and particles from pan on top of steak.

4. Scatter pickled onions on top of the plate. Crack some fresh pepper on top before serving. Serve with side of rice and enjoy!

CHEF'S TIP: Do not overcrowd your pan with too much beef when sauteeing, as this will produce too much juice in the pan and not allow the steak to caramalize.

For the pickled red onions

- 1 red onion, sliced thin
- 2 cups white vinegar
- 2 cups water
- 1 cup sugar
- 3 tablespoons salt

For the steak

- 1–2 pounds sirloin or ribeye steak, cut into 1- to 2-inch cubes
- 6 cloves garlic, smashed and diced into tiny pieces
- 2 tablespoons fish sauce (Chef Moy likes 3 Crab or Red Boat)
- 2 tablespoons soy sauce
- 2 tablespoons oyster sauce
- 2 tablespoons brown sugar
- Cracked pepper, to taste
- Oil for frying
- 1 small red onion, sliced into thin strips

For the finish

- 2 bunches of watercress
- 1 large tomato, sliced on the side
- Cracked pepper, to taste

ANDREW HEBERT

Portuguese culture and food are huge parts of the fabric of Boston. We should know, as one of us is of Portuguese ancestry, has made his own huge impact on the city, and knows what makes a Portuguese meal so special. The spices, the use of olive oil in all the best ways, the emphasis on fresh ingredients from land and sea, and pastries like flaky custard tarts (Pastéis de Nata) are flavors that the city is lucky to have. We are so awed by Chef Andrew Hebert's love letter to Portugal and Baleia in the South End, and the way he's encapsulated the feeling of being in a coastal Portuguese town as soon as you enter the Coda Group's latest restaurant.

The group behind Back Bay and South End's The Salty Pig, South End's SRV, and East Cambridge's Gufo teamed up with Chef Hebert in 2017. He served as the executive chef at The Salty Pig and Gufo before helming the kitchen at Baleia and becoming a restaurant partner. The Virginia native was no stranger to us or the Boston culinary scene, as he was Chef Jody Adam's protégé and worked in esteemed kitchens like Rialto, Trade, and Porto. His passion and the amount of care he puts into his craft was always evident, but his menu at Baleia, which is inspired from his trips to the Algarve and Lisbon, has elevated his culinary legacy even more.

We can tell Chef Hebert fell in love with the food from his travels when he uses the fresh seafood of New England but presents it in a traditional Portuguese way. Everything is deceptively simple; he showcases a few ingredients with a clean and elegant plating, but the bites are incredibly complex, surprising tastebuds while satisfying a craving of a place we'd love to visit. The grilled sardines drizzled with a turmeric chermoula sauce featuring North African spices is not to be missed. The Cataplana, which is a braised pork and seafood stew served in a copper bowl, is rich, comforting, and perfect for dipping bread in. Steamed baby clams in a vinho verde, cilantro, and lemon broth; Octopus Carpaccio served with crispy potato and a pimento aioli; and Salt Cod Bolinhos are just some of the small plates that guests can immerse themselves in, enjoying the coastal delights both New England and Portugal have to offer.

While the restaurant is seafood forward (the name Baleia means "whale" in Portuguese and gives a nod to whale watching in Portugal) and the nautical ambience boasts fish netting surrounding spherical lanterns from the ceiling as well as sailing ropes incorporated into the furniture, don't sleep on the fare from the land. One of the most popular dishes is the Piri Piri Chicken, warmly enveloped in a spicy sauce that only Chef Hebert and his team know the recipe to.

The wine list at Baleia exclusively features bottles from wineries in Portugal, and cocktails like white port tonics pair beautifully with the Mediterranean vibes. We were so happy to find Pastéis de Nata, baked cups of egg custardy creamy goodness, on the dessert menu. While Portuguese Sweet Rolls aren't technically dessert, we wouldn't mind having some at every point of the exceptional meal Chef Hebert has designed from a place that made such an impression on him. It's clear from his food that Portugal is a place that will always be on his mind and in his heart, and he has created a dining experience that Bostonians will never forget.

CHARRED CABBAGE "MOZAMBIQUE" WITH GARLIC, CHILI, AND CERVEJA

Serves 4

Mozambique sauce is a traditional sauce served with shrimp in Portuguese cuisine. This is a vegetarian version that even can be done vegan if the butter is omitted.

To make the piri piri sauce

1. Puree everything together with a blender. Simmer in a pan over medium-high heat for 5 minutes, stirring as needed.

To make the cabbage

1. Preheat the oven to 200°F. Coat the cabbage wedges in 3 tablespoons olive oil and salt. Sear them in a hot sauté pan or griddle for 4 to 5 minutes on each side, over medium-high heat, until the cabbage is brown and soft on the outside. Remove from the pan, and set the pan aside. Keep wedges in warm oven while finishing the cooking.

2. Allow the pan to cool slightly, then cook the garlic and shallot with the remaining olive oil in the same pan. Cook until the shallots are soft and the garlic is fragrant, about another 2 to 3 minutes. Then add the beer, piri piri sauce, butter, lemon juice, and cilantro, and bring everything to a boil.

3. Pour the pan sauce over the seared cabbage, and sprinkle the Aleppo chili over everything. Enjoy!

For the piri piri sauce

- 3 ounces Thai bird chili, stems removed (about 10 to 12)
- 3 ounces red fresno chili, stems and seeds removed (about 3)
- 1 red bell pepper, stems and seeds removed
- 2 cloves peeled garlic
- 2 tablespoons olive oil
- 1/2 teaspoon dry oregano
- 1 teaspoon smoked paprika
- 1 tablespoon pomegranate molasses

For the cabbage

- 1 large (or 2 small) heads of savoy cabbage, quartered into wedges with the core intact
- 3 tablespoons olive oil plus 2 tablespoons
- 1 teaspoon salt
- 6 cloves of garlic, sliced
- 1 large shallot or half an onion, thinly sliced
- 3 ounces (1/2 cup) Portuguese beer, or any European-style lager
- 1 tablespoon piri piri pepper sauce (you can add more if you want more heat)
- 2 tablespoon unsalted butter
- 1 tablespoon lemon juice
- 1 tablespoon cilantro, chopped
- 1/4 teaspoon Aleppo chili

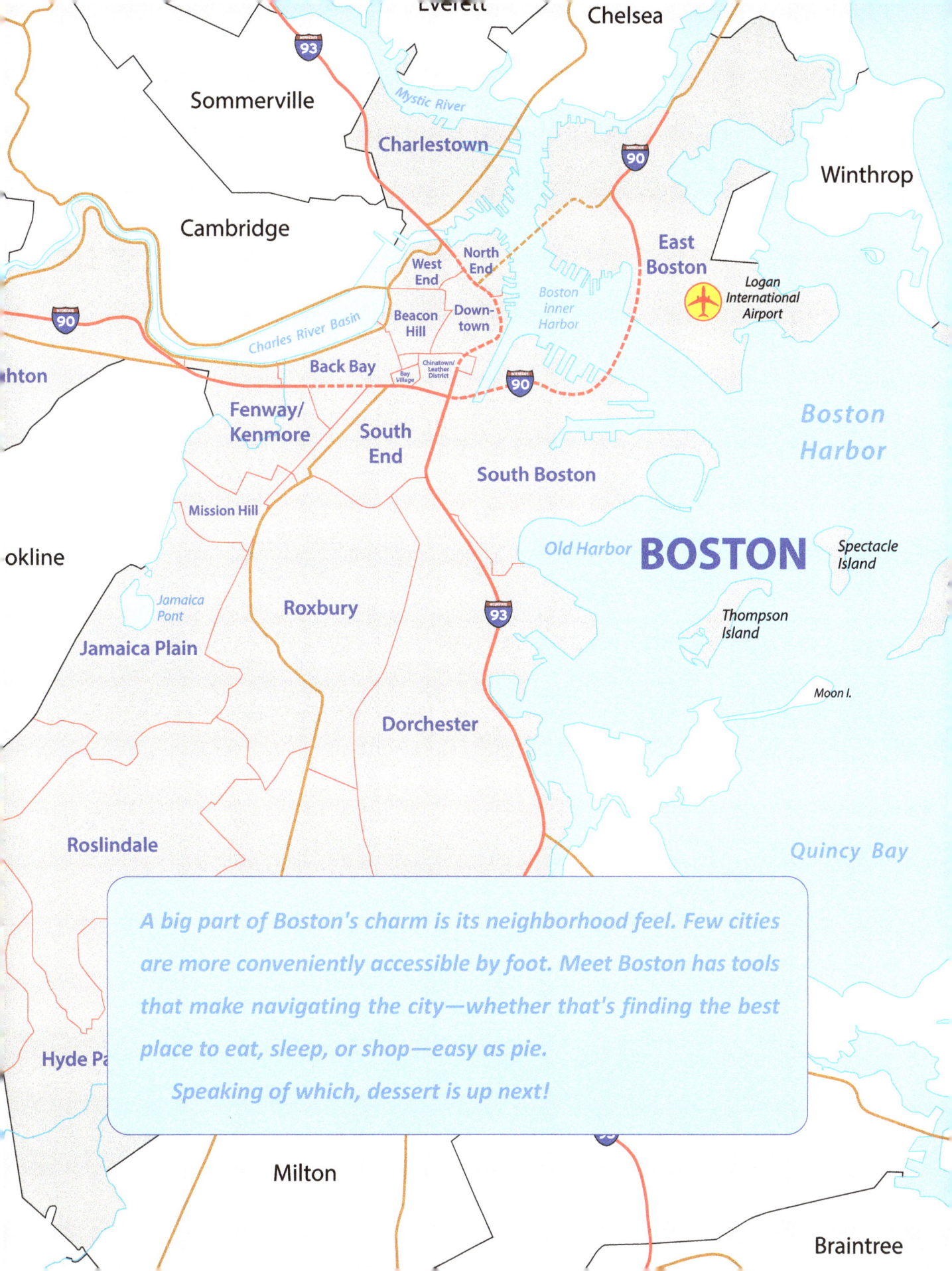

Dessert

JOANNE CHANG

We know people often say no one's perfect, but we're pretty sure Joanne Chang challenges that theory. The James Beard Award–winner for Outstanding Baker is the chef/co-owner of nine locations of Flour bakery, has written five successful cookbooks, and co-runs South End destination Myers + Chang with her husband, Christopher Myers. She graduated with honors from Harvard, has run sixteen Boston marathons, serves on the board of directors for Share Our Strength, and is a kind and gracious person with a million-dollar smile.

We know this is said a lot about people but, in Chang's case, truly, *we don't know how she does it.*

She grew up in Oklahoma and Texas in a traditional Taiwanese American household. Her mother cooked meals such as pork and chive dumplings, and Chang learned quickly that fresh ingredients make all the difference. Dessert, however, was not on the menu in her childhood home, except for the occasional orange or Toll House cookie, her mother's favorite treat.

Maybe that's why she became so good at making sweet treats, even before she opened a bakery.

Chef Chang came to Boston to study math and economics at Harvard. For fun, she'd bake cookies for friends and also sell cookies to a dorm grill on Harvard's campus. It didn't take her long to realize that the baking was what she wanted to do most of all.

She sent her resume to four chefs in the Boston area to see if she could find work in a kitchen. Chef Lydia Shire called her in, and Chang acquired experience at renowned restaurant Biba. Eventually she worked as pastry chef at Rialto, where she met restaurateur (and future husband) Christopher Myers.

In 2000 Chef Chang opened her own bakery, Flour, in the South End. She lived above it, waking up at 2:00 a.m., measuring everything to the gram, and brainstorming delectable cookies, cakes, tarts, sandwiches, and soups you wouldn't find anywhere else. Her sticky buns—which outshined Bobby Flay on *Throwdown with Bobby Flay*—are an example of how her math skills help craft the perfect baked good, but also how her love and care always create the perfect bite. She's one of the few who can probably quote all the numbers in pi while making a perfect pie.

Flour has locations in Back Bay, Beacon Hill, Cambridgeport, Central Square, Harvard Square, Fort Point, the Seaport, Hynes Convention Center, and South End, with their Breadquarters—yes, that's what Chang calls it—at the Boston Design Center. There are lines out the door at all locations. Her devotees flock to the stores for brown butter cinnamon rolls, vegan muffins, mile-high lemon meringue pie, and buttery croissants.

We love what she's done with her husband too. Myers + Chang, which opened in 2007, is one of our first recommendations to out-of-towners. We tell them to try the Asian fusion plates, such as the Hakka Eggplant or Black Pepper Surf & Turf Noodles. We also tell them they'll love the funky, inviting, creative restaurant that's a perfect blend of the couple behind it.

When we're at events with Chef Chang, we notice how everyone in the room, especially her peers, are so excited to speak with her. She always shows up with the utmost positivity, is full of grace, and is beloved by the industry and the city.

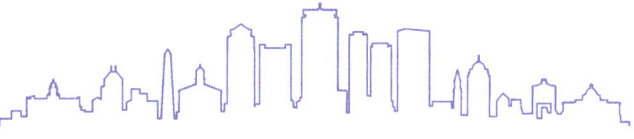

BOSTON CREAM PIE

Serves 4 to 6

A Boston classic that requires time, enthusiasm, and four to six loved ones to share this glorious dessert. Chef Chang's recipes always adds up to sweet results.

To make the pastry cream

1. In a medium saucepan, scald milk over medium-high heat (bubbles start to form around the edge of the pan, but the milk is not boiling).

2. While milk is heating, in a small bowl, stir together the sugar, flour, and salt. (Mixing the flour with the sugar prevents the flour from clumping when you add it to the egg yolks.)

3. In a medium bowl, whisk egg yolks until blended, then slowly whisk in the flour mixture. The mixture will be thick and pasty.

4. Remove milk from heat and slowly add it to the egg-flour mixture, a little at a time, whisking constantly. When all of the milk has been incorporated, return the contents of the bowl to the saucepan and place over medium heat. Whisk continuously and vigorously for about 3 minutes, or until the mixture thickens and comes to a boil. At first, the mixture will be very frothy and liquid; as it cooks longer, it will slowly start to thicken until the frothy bubbles disappear and it becomes more viscous. Once it thickens, stop whisking every few seconds to see if the mixture has come to a boil. If it has not, keep whisking vigorously. As soon as you see it bubbling, immediately go back to whisking for just 10 seconds, and then remove pan from heat. Boiling the mixture will thicken it and cook out the flour taste, but if you let it boil for longer than 10 seconds, the mixture can become grainy.

5. Pour/push/scrape the mixture through a fine-mesh sieve into a small, heatproof bowl. Stir in the vanilla and then cover with plastic wrap, placing it directly on the surface of the cream. This will prevent a skin from forming. Refrigerate for at least 4 hours, or until cold, or for up to 3 days in an airtight container.

To make the ganache

1. Place the chocolate in a small, heatproof bowl.

2. In a small saucepan over high heat, scald the cream (bringing it to just under a boil—bubbles will start to form around the edge of the pan but the cream should not come to a full boil).

3. Pour hot cream over chocolate and let sit for 30 seconds. Slowly whisk

For the pastry cream

1¼ cups milk

1/2 cup sugar

1/4 cup cake flour

1/2 teaspoon kosher salt

4 egg yolks

1 teaspoon vanilla extract

For the ganache

4 ounces semisweet or bittersweet chocolate (56 to 62 percent), chopped (or 3/4 cup semisweet or bittersweet chocolate chips)

1/2 cup heavy cream

For the cake

4 eggs, separated

1 cup sugar, divided

2 tablespoons lemon juice (about 1 lemon)

3 egg whites

3/4 cup unbleached all-purpose flour

1 pinch of kosher salt

1/4 cup hot coffee

1/4 cup sugar

1 cup heavy cream

(Continued)

chocolate and cream together until chocolate is completely melted and mixture is smooth.

4. Let cool to room temperature. The ganache can be stored in an airtight container in the refrigerator for up to 1 week.

To make the cake

1. Preheat to 350°F, placing rack in middle of the oven.

2. Line a 13- x 18-inch baking sheet with parchment paper. Cut a piece of cardboard into a 6- x 8-inch rectangle. Set aside. Using a stand mixer fitted with a whisk attachment (or a handheld mixer), beat together the 4 egg yolks, 1/4 cup sugar, and the lemon juice on high speed for 6 to 8 minutes (10 to 12 minutes with a handheld mixer) until thick and voluminous. Stop the mixer once or twice during whipping and scrape sides of bowl and whisk to make sure to get all the sugar and yolks to mix evenly. Transfer to a large bowl and set aside.

3. Clean the mixer bowl and the whisk attachment (they must be spotless) and fit the mixer with the whisk. Place the 4 egg whites plus the remaining 3 egg whites in the bowl and beat on medium speed for 1 to 2 minutes, or until they hold soft peaks. The whites will start to froth and turn into bubbles and eventually the yellowy viscous part will disappear. Keep whipping until you can see the tines of your whip leaving a slight trail in the whites. To test for the soft-peak stage, stop the mixer and lift the whip out of the whites; the whites should peak and then droop. (You may use a handheld mixer here as well; it will take a few extra minutes.)

4. On medium speed, add the remaining 3/4 cup sugar to the egg whites very slowly, taking about a full minute to add all the sugar. Whip on medium speed for another 2 to 3 minutes, or until the whites are glossy and shiny and hold a stiff peak when you slowly lift the whip straight up and out of the whites.

5. Using a rubber spatula, gently fold about 1/3 of the whipped whites into the yolk mixture to lighten it. Then gently fold in the remaining egg whites. Sift the flour and salt over the top of the mixture and fold in gently until the flour folds in completely. Spread the batter evenly in the prepared pan using an offset spatula to smooth the batter so it is even. Don't worry about the top being perfectly smooth; it is more important that the batter be spread evenly so the cakes are the same thickness throughout.

6. Bake for 18 to 24 minutes, rotating the cake pan once to ensure even baking, or until top springs back when pressed in the center with fingertips, the cake doesn't stick to your fingers, and the cake is pale golden brown. Let the cake cool in the pan for about 5 minutes.

CHEF'S TIP: Don't forget to rotate the cake pan when baking so everything is even and is that beautiful pale golden brown.

7. Run a paring knife around the edge of the cake to loosen it from the pan sides and invert the cake onto a cutting board. Gently peel off the parchment, and allow the cake to cool completely. Using a chef's knife, cut the sponge cake in half widthwise and then in half lengthwise; this will leave you with 4 rectangles, each about 5½ x 8 inches.

8. Stir together the hot coffee and sugar until the sugar is dissolved. Brush all 4 cake rectangles evenly with the coffee syrup, using up all of it. Place 1 cake quarter on the prepared cardboard rectangle. At this point you want to trim the cardboard so it's flush with the cake and is not jutting out unattractively from underneath the cake.

9. Whip heavy cream in a medium bowl until it holds firm, stiff peaks. Fold in previously prepared pastry cream until well combined. Using an offset spatula, spread about 1/3 of the pastry cream mixture evenly over the cake. There's a tendency for the cream to mound in the center, so be sure to spread the cream out to the edges of the cake. In fact, to make the best-looking cake possible, it's better for the cream layer to be slightly thicker along the edge than in the center.

10. Place a second cake layer on top of the cream and press down slightly to even out the cake so it is level. Using an offset spatula, spread about half of the remaining pastry cream mixture evenly over the cake. Again you want to spread the cream a bit thicker along the edge of the rectangle to prevent the final cake from doming.

11. Place a third cake layer on top of the cream and press down slightly to even out the cake so it's level. Using an offset spatula, spread the rest of the pastry cream mixture evenly over the cake, spreading it out so it's a bit thicker along the edges than in the center.

12. Top the cake with the final cake layer. Press down slightly to even out the cake so that the top layer is flat. Lightly drape the cake with plastic wrap and place in the freezer on a level surface and freeze until frozen solid, about 8 hours or overnight. (At this point the cake may be wrapped well in plastic wrap and stored in the freezer for up to 2 weeks.)

To finish

1. A few hours before serving, remove the cake from the freezer and place on a cutting board. Using a large chef's knife dipped in hot water, trim the edges of the cake so the edges are even and clean.

2. Place the cake on a rack with a baking tray underneath. Heat up the ganache until hot and pourable, and pour it carefully over the entire top of the cake. Spread the ganache on top so the chocolate layer is flat and even. Let the glaze drip down the sides.

3. Transfer cake to a serving plate. Let it defrost at room temp for about 2 hours or in the fridge for 4 hours or up to overnight before serving.

CHEF'S TIP: A few hours before serving, use a knife dipped in hot water to trim the edges of the cake once it's out of the freezer.

KATHY SIDELL AND BEN SIDELL

The effervescent restaurateur Kathy Sidell was always meant to be in the hospitality business, as the name Sidell *is* hospitality. It just took her a bit to lean into her destiny.

Her late father, Jack Sidell, was a banker who saw the potential in chefs like the late Jasper White, Lydia Shire, and Steve DiFillippo to name a few. She grew up with some of the most talented chefs cooking for her family and sharing in their stories. Without her father's foresight and belief in the chefs he supported, the Boston restaurant scene would not be what it is today.

Kathy's sister, Stephanie Sokolove, opened Newbury Street classic Stephanie's thirty years ago, which Kathy now owns. We don't know of any place that serves comfort food as authentic or as good as Stephanie's. Kathy credits her sister as her culinary inspiration and for being an excellent baker and cook who was ahead of her time. Kathy saw how her sister kept guests coming back year after year, and Kathy has done the same with her restaurants.

Before becoming a focal point of the Boston culinary scene, Kathy was a successful film producer. A graduate of Columbia film school, she'd traveled around the world making commercials, producing acclaimed documentaries, even being involved in music videos for artists like Nine Inch Nails. While film was a passion, so was food. A passion her father had passed down to her. We are so thankful that she embraced both art forms, as her influence in the city, especially for women, has been monumental.

Saltie Girl in Back Bay channels Kathy's memories of sailing in New England with her dad and their shared love of seafood. It's also inspired by Kathy's travels to Barcelona where she noticed wine bars were focusing on high-quality fish in tins. The menu at Saltie Girl is phenomenal, as all of Kathy's menus have been. With dishes like Lump Crab with Pistachios, Avocado, and Stracciatella on Toast; warm or cold New England lobster rolls; Fried Lobster and Waffles served with Sweet Corn Butter and Spicy Maple Syrup; and an extensive tin list featuring Grilled Branzino in Olive Oil from Italy or Smoked Salmon from Norway; it is a seafood lover's heaven.

Another heavenly part of the Saltie Girl menu are the desserts. The pastry chef had to be someone who was talented, who could revitalize the menu in new and fresh ways, and is someone Kathy has been a fan of for a long time. Her son, Ben Sidell, is behind Sweetboy desserts and has overseen and changed up the menus for Saltie Girl in Boston as well as in Los Angeles.

Much like his mother, Ben grew up in the hospitality scene and was surrounded by talented restaurateurs and chefs, but pursued one of his other passions first: acting. A graduate of USC and Harvard's MFA acting program, he would bake for family get-togethers between bookings. When he realized his baked goods were making his family and friends happy, he started Sweetboy Desserts out of his sister's home kitchen as a side business in 2019. His cookies, cakes, and Sweet Buns quickly earned him a following, and in 2022 he joined his mother and Saltie Girl culinary director Kyle McClelland to bring his Sweetboy ingenuity to the family business.

Ben's rotating creations are a sight to behold. His Sweetboy Chocolate Chip Cookie and the Strawberry & Raspberry Shortcake give guests a dopamine rush with every bite. The desserts at Saltie Girl give us as sweet a feeling, just like Kathy Sidell does. She's been a huge mentor to Tiffani Faison, to public relations maven Nicole Russo, and to Jenny, who adores Kathy and often asks her in person or over text how is she so innately happy? Kathy will always have a special place in Jenny's heart, not just because of who she is but because Jenny and her now husband Rob had a first date at one of Kathy's restaurants.

Kathy Sidell is the kind of person who, whether or not you're directly working with her, makes time for you, imparts wisdom, and is in the habit of giving all she can and then some. After all, she is her father's daughter.

PISTACHIO TIRAMISU

10 individual servings

Enjoy this delicious dessert on special occasions or even for when you crave a sweet treat midweek!

To make the lady fingers

1. Preheat oven to 325°F.

2. Whisk egg yolks and vanilla with 1/2 cup sugar until light and fluffy. In another bowl, whisk egg whites with the rest of the sugar until stiff peaks form. Fold the two into each other.

3. Add salt and sift the flour and baking powder into the mixture. Fold to incorporate.

4. Pipe 3-inch circles on a piece of parchment. Bake for 20 minutes. Cut the tops of the lady fingers off before using.

To make the pistachio cream

1. Whisk egg yolks and sugar until light and fluffy.

2. Beat mascarpone, pistachio paste, and salt until smooth. Fold both together.

3. Reserve in a piping bag.

To make the pistachio crunch

1. Toast pistachios. Mix butter, sugars, and water and cook over medium heat until the sugar is dissolved.

2. Turn up heat and cook to hard-crack stage (when read with a candy thermometer) until 305°f.

3. Remove from heat and add pistachios and vanilla.

4. Lay flat on a silicone mat, top with sea salt, and let cool. Then smash.

To make the mascarpone Chantilly

1. Hydrate gelatin. (Mix gelatin with water for about 10 minutes until it blooms.)

2. Heat half of the cream, sugar, and vanilla until it simmers. Remove and add gelatin.

3. Whisk until gelatin is melted. Pour over remainder of cream and mascarpone. Cover the top with plastic wrap and refrigerate 6 hours.

4. Whip and pipe.

For the lady fingers

- 6 egg yolks
- 2 teaspoons vanilla paste
- 1 cup sugar, divided
- 6 egg whites
- 1½ teaspoons salt
- 2½ cups gluten-free flour
- 1 teaspoon baking powder

For the pistachio cream

- 6 egg yolks
- 1/4 cup sugar
- 2 cups mascarpone
- 1/2 cup pistachio paste
- 1 teaspoon salt

For the pistachio crunch

- 1/4 cups grams chopped pistachio
- 1/2 cup (one stick) butter
- 4¾ tablespoons brown sugar
- 4 tablespoons sugar
- 4 tablespoons water
- 1/2 teaspoon vanilla extract
- 2 tablespoons sea salt

To finish

1. Pipe a layer of pistachio cream on the base of your cup/vessel.

2. Dunk one lady finger into the espresso mixture and lay on top of the pistachio cream.

3. Repeat steps 1 and 2.

4. Dome the top of the cup with mascarpone Chantilly and cover in smashed pistachio crunch. Enjoy!

For the mascarpone Chantilly

- 1 teaspoon gelatin
- 1 cup heavy cream
- 2 tablespoons powdered sugar
- 1/2 tablespoon vanilla paste
- 1/3 cup plus 1 tablespoon mascarpone
- 1 cup cold espresso with a splash of Mr. Black Coffee Liquor

CHEF'S TIP: If making ahead, once the top is covered in mascarpone Chantilly, cover in plastic wrap and refrigerate. Right before eating, remove the wrap and coat with pistachio crunch.

> **Billy:** I didn't think there was any way tiramisu could be made more delicious, but I learn something new every day.
>
> **Jenny:** What's not new is how impactful the Sidell family has been, and continues to be, to the culinary scene in Boston.

THE LENOX HOTEL

No matter how much Boston expands, to us, Back Bay Copley is the heartbeat of the city, and the Lenox Hotel is the boutique hotel that is an enormous part of that heartbeat. Dan Donohue is a steward of the city and, at the helm of a hotel that is first to respond to a crisis, gives philanthropically with events like their annual Room in Your Heart that fulfills the needs of families during the holiday season and is the true definition of hospitality. Jenny learned this firsthand when she was twenty-four and the apartment above hers caught fire. At an event with people representing the Lenox, Jenny's living situation came up in conversation. The Lenox folks asked her, "Why don't you come live with us?"

For three months, Jenny learned what hospitality of the highest order really entails from everyone who worked there. Jenny would be greeted every day, from the cleaning staff to the doormen to the bellhops, with a "Good Morning, Miss Johnson" or a "Good Evening, Miss Johnson." Everyone on the hotel staff became a friend who genuinely cared not just for Jenny, but for all their guests.

Jenny would joke that she felt a bit like Eloise from the picture book. When Jenny could return to her apartment, the entire staff who were so kind, signed a copy of Eloise for her. She still reads this book to her two daughters, Vienna and Lenox, who is named after a hotel that means so much. When Lenox sweetly asks when the family can go visit "her hotel" as they've done for holidays and other special occasions, Jenny gently reminds her that it's a hotel that's 100 percent there for everyone.

MAURA KILPATRICK

The goal of Sofra Bakery and Café in bustling Cambridge is to take guests to another place. Executive Pastry Chef and co-owner of Sofra, Maura Kilpatrick's desserts do just that by taking our tastebuds to nirvana with every bite.

The word *Sofra* loosely translates to "picnic" and the generosity and hospitality that comes with hosting *one. Th*e creations that Chef Kilpatrick oversees and bakes every day draw faithful crowds who would be happy to load their picnic blankets with everything her bakery has to offer.

Sofra is a collaboration between the Oleana Restaurant Group and Chefs Ana Sortun and Maura Kilpatrick. Together, they bring the diverse flavors of Turkey, Lebanon, Greece, and the Mediterranean to a relaxed café environment for Bostonians to savor. Chef Kilpatrick told us were it not for working with Chef Sortun, she would never have entered the world of Middle Eastern cuisine or learned about the flavors of the region. They opened Sofra in 2008 and continue to get rave reviews all these years later. The two even co-authored their successful cookbook *Soframiz: Vibrant Middle Eastern Recipes from Sofra Bakery.*

With a culinary background rooted in the California Culinary Academy, Kilpatrick honed her skills in San Francisco and Boston, collaborating with esteemed chefs like Lydia Shire, Rene Becker of Hi-Rise Bread Company, and Rene Michelena. Her reunion with Ana Sortun, following their previous collaboration at Moncef Meddeb's 8 Holyoke, led to her role as pastry chef at Oleana and the subsequent opening of Sofra.

Kilpatrick's expertise has earned her recognition from guests, critics, and peers alike, with multiple nominations by the James Beard Foundation for Outstanding Pastry Chef and Outstanding Baker. It's her experimentation with flavors of the East, the fun she has in mixing traditional technique with current tastes, and the way she consistently makes delectable works of art that make what she does so special.

In alignment with Sofra's commitment to sustainability, the café meticulously sources its ingredients, both locally and internationally, to ensure quality and freshness. There are excellent savory options to eat at Sofra, including Asparagus Phyllo Pie filled with herbed goat cheese, pistachio, and Greek garlic potato dip; Cheese Borek; Hot Lamb Moussaka; and Chicken Shawarma. There's a meze bar, retail goods, even prepared savory dishes to take home for dinner, such as Chicken Borani and Braised Greens or Stuffed Pepper Dolma.

However, we would be remiss if we didn't talk about the sweet stuff at Sofra. The Morning Bun made with croissant dough, cardamom, sugar, and orange blossom glaze is a must. From the Raspberry Rose Petal Turnover to the Pistachio Shortbread Cookies to the indulgent Walnut Baklava, each treat crafted by Kilpatrick and her team promises to satisfy any sweet craving, transporting taste buds to sublime realms of flavor.

SESAME CASHEW BAR

3 dozen bars

Our best seller, by far! It is a little tricky, because it actually comes out of the oven very under baked and sets up as it cools. But if it's cooked any longer, the caramel will be too hard and not chewy.

To make the crust

1. Line a 13- x 9-inch pan with foil, making sure it extends over all the sides. Very lightly spray or butter the foil.

2. Combine flour, sugar, salt, and cubed butter in food processor. Process 20 to 30 seconds until butter is in very small pieces, pulse more if needed.

3. Pour crust crumbs into prepared pan. Press into an even layer. Chill pan for 30 minutes. Crust can be prepared a day in advance.

4. Preheat oven to 350°F.

5. Bake crust for 25 minutes, until lightly browned.

To make the filling

1. Combine chopped cashews, sesame seeds, salt. Set aside.

2. Combine cream and vanilla separately.

3. Melt butter in medium saucepan. Add sugar, brown sugar, and honey. Heat over medium-high heat, whisking constantly, to dissolve sugar. Keep whisking for 2 to 3 minutes until caramel forms large bubbles and starts to thicken, or reaches 240°F on a candy thermometer. Remove from heat and whisk in cream and vanilla. Stir in cashews using a rubber spatula.

4. Pour on top of baked crust in even layer. Bake at 350°F for 26 to 28 minutes. The filling will appear unbaked. It should have bubbling caramel along the sides of the pan only and will still be liquid in center.

5. It will set up as it cools. It is very important not to overbake.

6. Cool completely.

7. It is best to wrap and refrigerate overnight and cut the next day if you can. Lift foil out of pan to remove. Remove foil. Cut into 1½-inch squares. Store in airtight container in refrigerator for up to 2 weeks.

For the crust

2 cups, plus 1 tablespoon flour

2/3 cup light brown sugar

1/2 teaspoon salt

14 tablespoons unsalted butter, chilled and cut into cubes

For the filling

3½ cups small chopped salted cashews

2 tablespoons sesame seeds

1/4 teaspoon salt

5 tablespoons heavy cream

1 teaspoon vanilla

2 sticks (1 cup) butter

1/4 cup sugar

1½ cups plus 2 tablespoons light brown sugar

1/2 cup honey

SARAH WADE

When our show caught up with Chef Sarah Wade at her Downtown restaurant, Stillwater, she told our audience an anecdote from earlier in her career. A male chef said to her once, "Your knife skills are okay, for a girl." This lit a fire inside of her. Whoever that chef is, we want you to take note of her beloved restaurants: Stillwater, The Mac Bar inside of Stillwater, and Sloane's in Allston. How are her knife skills now, bro?

Stillwater is a result of a promise Chef Wade made to herself and the audience of the Food Network's *Chopped Gold Medal Games*, when she won the competition in 2018. She said that with the prize money she would open her own restaurant. From what we've learned about the talented and funny Chef Wade, she keeps her promises.

Chef Wade grew up in Edmond, Oklahoma, where she worked as a barista in a local coffee shop as a teenager. She graduated from Oklahoma State University's School of Hotel and Restaurant Administration, which made such an impression on her, she named her restaurant Stillwater after the town the university is in.

She'd had positions as banquet chef and sous chef with the Renaissance Hotels in Houston, Texas, and Charlotte, North Carolina; was executive chef for the Marriott Energy Corridor in Houston and for the Hyatt Regency in New York and Connecticut, but when she answered an ad to helm Lulu's in Allston, Chef Wade finally felt like she had found her home.

She started at Lulu's in 2014, and her reputation and menu put her on many Best Brunch lists as well as winning her the 2016 Boston Brunch Battle. It also earned a call from *Chopped* producers. Since winning the competition, Chef Wade has specialized in food from her childhood that make her feel good, and she wants guests to take part in the "warm and fuzzies" of her comfort food creations.

Stillwater opened in 2019 and the heavenly aromas of Chef Wade's Smoked Pork Mac & Cheese have lured many eager guests inside. Her homemade Cheese-its—served with a cucumber dill dip—and Chicken Fried Rib-Eye are just some of Chef Wade's creative comfort offerings, but her desserts really bring the warm and fuzzies.

The Signature PB&J Crème Brûlée, Lemon Cheesecake, and Chocolate Caramel Cake are all decadently divine. Her S'Mores Donuts really take the cake (err . . . donut in this case!). She's offered her highly coveted recipe for ricotta donuts here, which you'll want some more of with or without marshmallow fluff and chocolate sauce.

RICOTTA DONUTS WITH HONEY RUM SAUCE

Makes about 12 donuts

Nice and fluffy, these donuts give the warm fuzzies on their own. When dipped in honey rum sauce, they are vessels of pure joy.

To make the donuts

1. Mix together flour, sugar, and baking powder, and set aside.

2. In a stand mixer, whip together ricotta, eggs, salt, vanilla, and orange zest.

3. Add in 1/4 of the mixed dry ingredients and mix on low. Continue to add the dry ingredients until fully incorporated. It will be very stiff. Do not over mix. Let dough rest for 10 to 15 minutes.

4. Warm oil in a Dutch oven to 350°F.

5. Working in batches, use a 1-ounce cookie scoop to scoop and drop dough into oil. It's best to cook 6 to 8 donuts at a time. Let them cook for 7 to 8 minutes, moving them around occasionally to make sure they cook evenly on all sides.

6. While donuts are cooking, add powdered sugar to mixing bowl. When donuts are done cooking, pull them out of the pot, give them a quick shake, and put directly into powdered sugar. Shake around to coat completely. Put on a plate.

To make the honey rum sauce

7. In a small pot, bring honey, butter, rum, and salt to a simmer. Remove and pour into a small dish for dipping.

---

1 cup all-purpose flour
3 tablespoons granulated sugar
2 teaspoons baking powder
1 cup ricotta cheese
2 large eggs
1 pinch of salt
1 teaspoon vanilla paste
Zest of one orange
Canola oil for frying
1 cup powdered sugar

For the honey rum sauce

1/4 cup honey
1 tablespoon butter
2 tablespoons dark rum
Pinch of salt

RACHEL SUNDET

It's a family affair at Big Dipper Hospitality. The restaurant group consists of seven owners, including three couples: Alon Munzer and Rachel Miller-Munzer, Heather Mojer and Evan Harrison, Rachel and Tyler Sundet, and John Kessen. When we heard this, it sounded like there may be too many cooks in the kitchen (pun very intended). But the team works so well together and has created the very special Mamaleh's Delicatessen and Restaurant with locations in Cambridge, Brookline, and Downtown Crossing.

The Big Dipper Group was already involved in the restaurant business as individuals before joining forces, but they had a collective dream to bring a Jewish deli experience to Boston proper. *Mamaleh* is a Yiddish term of endearment for kids, like calling a young girl a "little mama." Mamaleh's, which opened in 2016, is named for the group's children and is dedicated to their growing families (we counted eight at their ribbon-cutting ceremony for their new Mamaleh's Kibitz Corner event space in Cambridge).

When one of us eats at Mamaleh's, it tastes like her childhood. Getting to eat food that Jenny would have at high holidays brings so many beautiful memories to the surface; it's just like eating her beloved late grandmother's food. When Billy goes with Jenny to Mamaleh's, he finds it impossible not to marvel at how much chopped liver Jenny can consume. It delights him to see her have a smile from the food every time they visit, even when she gets a little schmutz on her face from overexcitement.

There are people of all cultures and faiths noshing at Mamaleh's because good food is for everybody and Mamaleh's welcomes everyone. The menu at Mamaleh's has a lot of staples like matzah ball soup, pastrami Reuben sandwiches, and whitefish salad or Nova lox on bagels, but there are more creative interpretations of these deli classics as well. The Leo breakfast sandwich has lox, scrambled eggs, onion, and dill mayo on a challah roll; there's a Smoked Mushroom Rachel sandwich with portobello mushrooms with all the trimmings on seeded rye for vegetarians; and the baked goods . . . well they're exceptional.

All of the bagels, challah, babka, bialys, muffins, cookies, rugelach, and more are made in Mamaleh's bakery, and chef and part-owner Rachel Sundet is in charge. Her first restaurant kitchen job was at Amanda Lydon and Susan Regis's Upstairs on the Square. Chef Sundet says they set the tone for the kind of chef she wanted to be, and she was grateful to have two talented female chefs as role models.

She was named Best Pastry Chef by *Boston* magazine in 2015, and her work at Mamaleh's is astounding. Her flaky Raspberry Walnut Rugelach, Sesame Tahini Cookie, and Halvah Chocolate Chunk Banana Muffins are so delicious, it would be a shanda not to try them. The warmth from Chef Sundet's baked goods matches the warm feeling we get every time we visit Mamaleh's.

HONEY CAKE

3 8-inch loaf pans or 1 bundt pan

A moist, lightly caramelized cake rich in history with origins going back centuries, this dessert symbolizes the sweetness to come in the new year during Rosh Hashanah celebrations, but can be enjoyed anytime.

1. Preheat oven to 325°F.
2. Spray pan(s) with nonstick.
3. In a large bowl, whisk the flour, baking powder, baking soda, sugars, and spices together.
4. In a separate bowl, mix the rest of the ingredients together.
5. Making a well in the dry ingredients. Add the wet ingredients in three batches, whisking from the center out to incorporate the dry ingredients and avoid lumps.
6. Whisk together well and scrape the bottom and sides of the bowl to make sure the batter is smooth and consistent.
7. Divide the batter between the three loaf pans or pour it all into the bundt pan.
8. Bake for 35 to 40 minutes, rotating the pans halfway through the baking. You're looking for the cake to be domed slightly, pulling away from the sides of the pan. It should be springy to the touch on top and a rich brown color.
9. Once baked, let cake cool on a wire rack.
10. While still warm, brush with warmed honey on top.

3¼ cups all-purpose flour
1 teaspoon baking powder
1 teaspoon baking soda
1⅓ cups sugar
1/2 cup light brown sugar
1 teaspoon kosher salt
2 teaspoons ground cinnamon
1/2 teaspoon ground cloves
1/2 teaspoon ground allspice
1/4 teaspoon ground white pepper
1/4 teaspoon ground cardamom
1 cup sunflower oil (vegetable)
1 cup honey
3 whole eggs, room temperature
1 cup Earl Grey tea, strong (steeped 10 to 30 minutes)
1/2 cup fresh orange juice
1/4 cup Mahia Brandy (fig and juniper, but you can sub in any kind of brandy)

CHEF'S TIP: This cake freezes well, just slack overnight and refresh with a drizzle of warm honey.

RENAE CONNOLLY AND MICHAEL PAGLIARINI

When Chef Michael Pagliarini explains to us one of his dishes and speaks about each ingredient with such cerebral thoughtfulness, we can imagine the flavors even before he puts the plate in front of us. He's worked with the likes of Gordon Hamersley, Michael Schlow, and Grant Achatz, and his devotion to his craft and the artful display of the meals he creates are unparalleled and transcendent. The chef/owner of Giulia and Moëca, both in Cambridge, is intentional and respectful of all of his seasonally available ingredients. The same can be said about his staff, and especially true of Moëca's Pastry Chef, Renae Connolly.

Chef Connolly grew up in Fresno, California, and as a teen worked at a local bakery. Starting as a dishwasher, then moving up to assistant baker, she set her sights on the California Culinary Academy in San Francisco. She came to Boston to work at Ken Oringer's Clio and was mentored by Pastry Chef Rick Billings who taught her a plethora of techniques she still uses today.

Her reputation grew as she worked at other restaurants in New York and Boston. Her partnership with Chef Pagliarini is a great fit. Their mutual respect for one another, their shared love of ingredients, and their meticulous attention to detail, make their pairing a sweet one.

A Taste of Boston

Moëca specializes in seafood sourced from small-boat fishermen around the world. The menu continues to evolve with fresh and delicious dishes that are also responsible. While Barbequed Mussels served with beet molasses and hazelnut satay as well as Battered Halibut served with vermouth, peas, and caviar are huge draws, the dessert at Moëca is a star all its own.

We always marvel at what James Beard semi-finalist of 2018 Chef Connolly comes up with. Each of her desserts is breathtakingly detailed and colorful, but we sometimes get a little sad knowing that our favorite dessert might be out of rotation. The Miso Chocolate Bread Pudding topped with sesame candied cashews, roasted banana, nyangbo nemelaka, and lavender chocolate gelato was a stunner; as was her Sunflower Mousse with rhubarb jam, dukkah honeycomb crunch, and ginger gelato. But it's her cakes that are so swoony that we wish we had more than one stomach!

Boston magazine named her Best Pastry Chef of 2023, but to her husband and son, Renae is also best wife and mother. We think she has a great energy and is one of the most talented pastry chefs on the planet, and not just because she was able to guide Billy through baking gooey chocolate cakes on our show during one of her first ever TV appearances.

GOOEY CHOCOLATE CAKES WITH RICOTTA FROSTING

8 4-ounce cakes

Chef Connolly showed Billy how to make these delicious gooey chocolate cakes on television. It's one of her favorite recipes—super decadent and luscious—and is friendly for the home baker.

To make the ricotta frosting

1. Measure the ricotta into a medium mixing bowl and set aside.

2. Measure the cream, sugar, vanilla, and orange blossom water into a different medium-size bowl. Whisk the mixture until the cream reaches soft peaks. Be careful not to overwhip!

3. Switching to a rubber spatula, fold half the cream into ricotta, mixing gently. Add the remaining cream to the bowl and fold together until it becomes a homogenous mixture.

4. Cover with plastic or beeswax wrap and cool in the fridge for a minimum of 30 minutes.

To make the cakes

1. Preheat oven to 325°F.

2. Fill a medium pot a third of the way with water and bring to a simmer.

3. In a medium-size mixing bowl, measure your butter, sugar, and chocolate. Place the bowl in the pot of hot water and let everything completely melt.

4. Whisk the whole eggs and yolks together so they are liquid and smooth, set aside.

5. Mix the flour, salt, and baking powder together and set aside.

6. Using either butter or pan spray, grease 8 4-ounce baking ramekins and set aside.

7. Once chocolate mixture is melted, remove the bowl from the heat and set it on a towel to catch any dripping water. Watch out for steam as you lift the bowl out of the pot.

8. Using a whisk, quickly stream in the eggs and stir rapidly. Once eggs are fully incorporated, whisk in the flour mixture. The batter should be shiny and lump free. If you have an immersion stick blender, you can buzz the batter to remove any lumps.

For the ricotta frosting

- 1¼ cup fresh ricotta
- 1/3 cup plus 3 tablespoons heavy cream
- 1/2 cup powdered sugar
- 1/2 teaspoon vanilla extract
- 1/2 teaspoon orange blossom water (optional)
- 1 pinch of salt

For the cakes

- 1 cup unsalted butter
- 1/2 cup sugar
- 1 cup dark chocolate of choice (Chef Connolly loves Valrhona Al Paco 66 percent, but any bittersweet dark chocolate will do!)
- 4 whole eggs
- 4 egg yolks
- 4 teaspoons all-purpose flour
- 1/4 teaspoon salt
- 1/8 teaspoon baking powder

For the finish

Fresh berries, optional

9. Fill your greased ramekins three quarters of the way full. Bake for 8 to 15 minutes. When done, the cakes will rise on the edges but still look soft and gooey in the center. You will see the batter change from shiny and wet to a matte finish on the top. If it looks a little wet, leave them in the oven for 1 more minute.

10. Remove and allow to cool.

To assemble

1. Slightly warm the chocolate cakes in the oven or microwave. You can flip the cakes out onto a plate or serve them in the ramekins.

2. Scoop a heaping dollop of ricotta frosting on top of the cake and garnish with some fresh berries.

> **Jenny:** What do you think, Bill? One of the most delicious desserts ever?
>
> **Billy:** And the gooiest!

HOLLY SAFFORD

If there is a major event in the city of Boston, we can be sure that Holly Safford's The Catered Affair is responsible for the exceptional food, the above and beyond hospitality, and for making sure every event they take care of leads to a lifetime of memories.

We know firsthand her and her staff's level of commitment to guests, as The Catered Affair was there for Jenny and Rob's wedding at the Boston Public Library. With a keen eye for design, decades of experience, and a genuine passion for her work, Holly ensures that every occasion becomes a cherished memory. Holly Safford acted as a guide for Jenny and her wedding party and helped create the most magical moment in any bride and groom's life.

One of the most sought after and largest independently owned catering companies, The Catered Affair began in 1979. Holly was going through a divorce and had to figure out what the next chapter of her life would look like while raising three young sons. Her friends mentioned how much they loved get-togethers at Holly's home and encouraged her to get into the catering business. What started with a four-slice toaster oven, a station wagon for transport, a few silver trays, and belief in herself turned into a nationally recognized company with hundreds of employees in multiple locations catering all over New England.

As word of mouth spread about The Catered Affair, Holly was hired for more prestigious events, but she's treated every event with the same amount of care. She's always strived to make each event unique. Her food is literally art for the senses, carefully customized to each of her client's needs.

Whether it was an event for former Governor Dukakis, the late Senator Ted Kennedy, heads of state like the late Nelson Mandela, then-Prince Charles, or Michelle Obama, if there was a distinguished guest coming to Boston, the event coordinators knew they were in good hands with The Catered Affair.

Her culinary pedigree is so trusted, Julia Child asked her to write recipe articles on Julia's behalf for *Parade* magazine. The two formed a close friendship, and Holly credits Julia Child as being one of her greatest mentors in Boston. If you'd like to try some of Holly and her staff's tasty offerings but don't have a social event on the calendar, not to worry. The Catered Affair experience can be found in tea rooms, restaurants, and cafés at the Boston Public Library, Harvard Art Museums, The Institute of Contemporary Art, and The Boston Athenaeum.

The Catered Affair is a family affair with Holly's sons, Andrew and Alex, building upon the business. She's been the consummate hostess in Boston, not just because of the excellent events she's created, but because of her deep involvement in the community. She's partnered with organizations like The Greater Boston Food Bank, The Boys & Girls Club of Boston, and Neighborhood House Charter School to name a few. Through her philanthropy and unwavering dedication, Holly Safford has solidified her legacy as the epitome of excellence in the catering industry.

ESPRESSO MARTINI COCONUT MACAROONS

20 macaroons

Chef Safford's Espresso Martini Coconut Macaroons will be a hit at any event whether you're hosting a cocktail party, a wedding, or an afternoon tea.

1. Preheat the oven to 325°F.

2. Combine coconut, condensed milk, espresso powder, pure vanilla extract, and Kahlúa in a large bowl.

3. In the bowl of an electric mixer fitted with the whisk attachment, whip egg whites and salt on high speed until they make medium-firm peaks. Carefully fold the egg whites into the coconut mixture.

4. Using a sorbet scoop (or 2 teaspoons), drop the batter onto sheet pans lined with parchment paper. Bake for 20 to 25 minutes, until golden brown.

5. Place 3/4 of the chocolate in a double boiler over simmering water. Stir frequently, scraping down the sides with a rubber spatula until chocolate melts, about 5 minutes. Remove from heat and stir in the rest of the chocolate until it melts.

6. While the chocolate is still liquid, dip the base of each cooled macaroon about 1/8 inch into the chocolate. Place cookies, chocolate-side down, on parchment paper. Let the chocolate harden completely before serving.

- 14 ounces sweetened flaked coconut
- 14 ounces fat-free condensed milk
- 1 tablespoon espresso powder
- 1 teaspoon pure vanilla extract
- 2 teaspoons Kahlúa
- 2 extra-large egg whites, room temperature
- 1/4 teaspoon kosher salt
- 4 ounces semi-sweet chocolate bits

Side Dish

BOSTON PUBLIC LIBRARY

The Boston Public Library (BPL) stands as an enchanting blend of the city's rich history and its forward trajectory. Since its establishment in 1848, it has proudly held the distinction of being the first large, free municipal library in the US. The iconic Dartmouth Street building dates back to 1895. Meanwhile, the McKim building in Copley Square, adorned with gorgeous European and Italian architecture and grand murals, has earned its status as a national historic landmark.

In 2016 the Boylston Street building underwent a major renovation and now boasts an ultra-modern lecture hall, a new children's library, a dedicated teen space, and even a WGBH satellite broadcast station, offering guests a rare opportunity to listen to broadcasts in real time.

A perennial favorite among locals and visitors alike, the BPL boasts one of the country's largest collections, housing an impressive array of twenty-three million items, ranging from books and drawings to maps and original music scores by luminaries like Mozart. It's also home to fabulous places to eat, including the Map Room Tea Lounge, The Courtyard Restaurant, and the Newsfeed Café, all supplied with exquisite food from Holly Safford's The Catered Affair.

Photos by Hancer Photography

There's nothing more grand or beautiful than the courtyard at the BPL. Especially when Jenny and Rob had their wedding there, as it's a special place for both of them. It's where Rob wrote his first book and a place they both actively support. As the carving on the façade of the Copley building says, the library is "Free to All." Always has been, and always will be for future generations.

A Taste of Boston

ABDULLA AWAD

We *love* baklava, which is why we had to check out Yafa Bakery & Café in Somerville, named Best New Bakery of 2023 by *Boston* magazine.

After visiting—and featuring Yafa on our show—we can confirm: This place is excellent.

When you enter, you're welcomed by the aromas of fresh-baked bread and *kunafah*, a beautiful blend of pastry and cheese. You might also be invited in by owner and creator Abdulla Awad himself, whose megawatt smile can brighten any Boston day. Play your cards right and you might get a complimentary cup of cardamom spiced chai or sweet and minty lemonada.

This is just what Abdulla does. Once you're a customer, you're part of the Yafa family.

Abdulla Awad doesn't consider himself a chef, but he agrees he's an artist. In Abdulla's native Jerusalem, he often heard the saying, "The eye eats before the mouth." Every piece of food that comes out of what Yafa calls his "culinary art lab" is a feast for the eyes as well as the stomach. When you see the level of detail in his pastries and savory breads, you'll understand his and his staff's commitment to the artistry of his baked goods. They want everything to be "artfully delicious," which is the motto of the bakery/café.

Yafa means "beautiful" in both Aramaic and in Hebrew. In Arabic it's the name of one of the oldest cities in the world, about forty-five minutes from where Abdulla grew up. One of six siblings in a Palestinian family, his father owned a grocery store, and his mother cooked every day, not only for her family but for neighbors and members of the community. Awad says his mother is just as talented as chefs from the most elite culinary schools in the world, and because we've tried his take on her recipes, we believe him.

If you want to go the savory route at Yafa, go for the Spinach and Cheese Snail or Safayeh Yafaweyah, a phyllo dough spiral filled with spinach, feta, ricotta, onions, olive oil from Jerusalem, dill, sea salt, and black pepper baked to a perfect golden hue. Another customer favorite is the Jerusalem bread, which is a freshly baked oval topped with toasted sesame seeds. Perfect for dipping into baba ghanoush or labneh!

If you're like us—well, Jenny mostly—and have a bit of a sweet tooth but don't want things too sweet, the Medjool dates, which are imported from Jericho, are your best bet. They remove the pits from the dates and fill them with different flavor combinations. Some dates are covered in chocolate, others are gorgeously decorated with twenty-four-karat golden leaf dust, each a gem that makes us feel like we've gone the regal yet healthy route for a sweet treat.

But if we *really* want to indulge our sweet tooth, the only thing sweeter than Abdulla Awad's hospitality is the baklava, adorned with rose petals and pistachios.

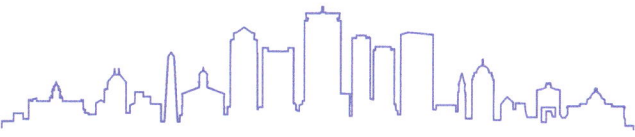

ALMONDO

Makes 22-25 pieces

Artfully delicious in every way, this Almondo is sure to be a feast for the eyes as well as the mouth.

1. In a blender, combine the butter, oil, baking powder, cornstarch, egg, sugar, and vanilla until well blended.

2. Gradually add flour until dough is firm enough to hold but not overly oily. Allow dough to rest in refrigerator for about 20 minutes.

3. Preheat oven to 350°F.

4. Shape dough into finger-size pieces, maintaining a thickness not too thin or thick.

5. Place shaped dough on a baking sheet lined with parchment paper.

6. Bake cookies for 10 to 12 minutes, or until they achieve a golden color, not too crisp and not too soft.

7. Allow cookies to cool completely. For best results, freeze cookies overnight to ensure they maintain the desired texture during the coating process.

8. Dip each cookie into the melted white chocolate, ensuring it is completely coated.

9. Roll chocolate-coated cookie in almonds, ensuring an even coating.

10. Allow cookies to set on a parchment-lined surface.

- 1 pound white chocolate, melted
- 2 cups fine-ground roasted almonds, toasted
- 1 cup unsalted butter
- 1/2 cup vegetable oil
- 1/2 tablespoon baking powder
- 1/2 cup cornstarch
- 1 egg
- 1/4 cup cane sugar
- 1 teaspoon vanilla extract
- 4 cups all-purpose flour

WILL GILSON AND BRIAN MERCURY

When chef and restaurateur Will Gilson, one of the most-liked chefs around, opens a restaurant, we know it will be around for a long time. With a total commitment to quality and a deep-rooted connection to New England's culinary heritage, his Cambridge Street Hospitality Group restaurants consistently provide exceptional dining experiences that leave a lasting impression on guests. He is as New England and as farm-to-table as it gets. His family history dates back to the Plymouth pilgrims, and he was raised on his family's herb farm. All of this has led him to focus on the best New England has to offer and lay the foundation for his culinary philosophy.

Gilson's dining destinations are all stellar, but they all offer something different. Puritan & Company, the flagship establishment, showcases modern American cuisine infused with traditional New England flavors, reflecting Gilson's deep-seated roots. Puritan Oyster Bar entices with a selection of seafood delights, while The Lexington Roof Deck and Bar offers views coupled with expertly crafted dishes. Gepetto, Gilson's homage to Italian cuisine, celebrates the bounty of New England's land and sea. Completing the lineup is Café Beatrice, a haven for artisanal pastries and gourmet sandwiches.

An essential collaborator in Gilson's culinary ventures is Pastry Chef Brian Mercury. He's in charge of all things sugar, and his confectionery creations elevate all of the Cambridge Street Hospitality dining experiences to new heights.

Hailing from Rochester, New York, Chef Mercury's passion for pastry was nurtured in his grandmother's kitchen, helping her bake desserts and cookies. His first job in Boston was working at The Charles Hotel with Chefs Peter Davis and Dan Angelopolus. He told us he's forever grateful to these mentors for teaching him what it meant to work hard and have passion for what he makes. His work experience continued at Harvest, where *Boston* magazine named him Boston's Best Pastry Chef 2014, and at Oak + Rowan in his role as executive pastry chef.

The desserts he makes for Cambridge Street Hospitality Group are astounding. His Peanut Butter Breakfast Cookie, Passionfruit Brioche, Cinnamon Roll, and Cherry and Apricot Cheese Puff frustrate us because sometimes after a meal at Puritan & Company, we only have room for one of his creations. His desserts make to-go boxes one of the greatest innovations in human history.

The desserts at Gepetto are ridiculously artistic and seasonally inspired. Chef Mercury's Rhubarb Buttermilk Tart with ricotta mousse, Meyer marmalade, and bay leaf dust are the stuff dreams are made of, and his plating of his creations show his sense of design is as immaculate as his way with flavors.

The two chefs have helped make Inman Square in Cambridge a culinary destination, and their harmonious blend of taste and aesthetics in their food is as impressive a combination as they are. Another sweet thing about them? Seeing them at charity events we've emceed over the years and their willingness to give back to organizations like Spoonfuls.

PISTACHIO CITRUS CHEESECAKE

1 10-inch cheesecake

This Pistachio Citrus Cheesecake is creative, zesty, creamy, and smooth. It's a dessert for the ages that will be a go-to recipe in your family for years to come. It is important that all of these ingredients be at room temperature to keep the cake from cracking.

1. Preheat oven to 325°F.
2. With a fork, combine graham crumbs and melted butter until mixture holds its shape when pressed in your hand, and no dried crumbs are visible.
3. Spray a 10-inch, high-sided cake pan or spring form pan with pan spray and line bottom with a parchment paper circle.
4. Press in graham cracker bottom and bake in oven for 8 minutes, set aside to cool.
5. Once cool, wrap the bottom of the pan with aluminum foil.
6. Once ready to make your batter, make sure all the ingredients are room temperature before starting, this prevents cake from cracking.
7. In a standing mixer combine cream cheese and sugar in mixer with paddle attachment, and mix until smooth.
8. Turn mixer to medium-low speed, as you will have a lot of batter. Add in pistachio paste, sour cream, eggs, salt, zest, and spices. Mix well, scraping sides and bottom of bowl occasionally.
9. Add in heavy cream.
10. Place the pan on a rimmed baking sheet. Re-spray sides of pan and pour batter over toasted graham cracker base. Add water to the baking sheet, and bake cake in the water bath 1½ to 2 hours or until it has a firm jiggle when pressed in center and is golden around the edges.
11. Cool to room temperature on a wire rack.
12. Fully refrigerate before serving.
13. Unmold, transfer to a serving plate, and top as desired.

- 1½ cups graham cracker crumbs
- 1/2 cup (8 tablespoons) butter, melted
- 3 pounds cream cheese (6 8-ounce bars)
- 2⅓ cup sugar
- 1 cup pistachio paste (you can find online or in specialty shops)
- 1 cup, plus 1 tablespoon sour cream
- 9 eggs
- 1/2 teaspoon salt
- 3 oranges, zested
- 1 tablespoon ground coriander
- 1 cup heavy cream

JULIE FREITAS

In the Greater Boston area, when someone mentions brambles, we know they're not talking about thorny bushes; they're craving the scrumptious, flaky pockets of pie filled with raspberry jam from Sugar Baking Company in West Roxbury. At this haven where "sweet things happen," brambles are just the beginning.

There's nothing too sweet for Sugar Baking Company because they do everything. For breakfast, indulge in savory and sweet croissants, apple and raspberry danishes, scones, muffins, and teacakes that vary daily. Weekends bring fresh cinnamon rolls and donuts, satisfying every craving.

As for desserts, the options are endless. Cupcakes like the Black Magic, filled with chocolate pudding and dipped in chocolate ganache, change daily. Italian pastries like Zeppoli and Ricotta Pie slices save you a trip to the North End. Tarts, brownies, apple bear claws, turnovers, bread pudding, whatever your sweet tooth craves, they've got it. And don't get us started on all the cookies! Hermits, coconut macaroons, and yes, brambles, which you can order by the pound.

Continuing the sweet tradition started by Eric Battite and his family, is the new owner of Sugar Baking Company, Julie Freitas. She tells us that her passion for baking comes from her mom and her nana, who were dedicated to preserving the family's culinary heritage, especially during the holidays. At Christmas, she loved smelling her mom's Bishop's bread in the oven while her nana made holiday jelly. These warm memories are some of her sweetest, and she wants to help make sweet memories for others with her baked goods.

Before Freitas took over Sugar Baking Company, she started her own vegan baked donut business, Planted Donuts, in 2021. Her dream was to make the most exquisite donuts in the most compassionate way. She started the business using the Revolving Test Kitchen, a shared culinary workspace in Lawrence, Massachusetts, to make that dream come true.

Julie Freitas's sweet dreams continue as she carries on Sugar Baking Company's legacy. She knows the responsibility. She has been entrusted with the local legend that is the bramble, and she won't let our sweet tooths down.

SUGAR BAKING CO. HERMITS

2 logs

A New England dessert since the 1800s, this chewy tradition is in good hands with Chef Julie Freitas. She helps you carry on the tradition, no matter where you live, with this fantastic recipe.

1. Preheat oven to 350°F.
2. Cream butter, shortening, sugars, and molasses until light and fluffy.
3. Add egg, mix until combined. Scrape down sides and bottom of bowl.
4. In a separate bowl, mix together remaining dry ingredients. Add to mixer. When combined, turn onto medium speed and allow to mix for 3 to 5 minutes.
5. Add raisins and mix just until combined.
6. Line sheet pan with parchment paper.
7. Transfer hermit mixture into piping bag. Cut hole roughly the size of a half dollar.
8. Pipe hermit, longways, from end to end on the sheet pan. Logs should be about 2 inches wide.
9. Bake for 10 to 15 minutes. Hermits should be a nice and even rich brown color.
10. Let cool and cut however you like to serve.

1½ ounces butter, softened
2½ ounces shortening
3 ounces light brown sugar
2½ ounces granulated sugar
3 tablespoons molasses
1 egg
1½ teaspoons baking soda
1/4, plus 1/8 teaspoons salt
7½ ounces cake flour
2 tablespoons bran
1/4 tablespoon cinnamon
3/4 teaspoons ginger
1/4, plus 1/8 teaspoons clove
1/2 cup raisins

JENNY JOHNSON

Photo by Mike Diskin

Jenny Johnson is a three-time Emmy Award-winning executive producer and on-air talent. Born in Boston, raised in Worcester and then in Marblehead, Johnson graduated from the University of New Hampshire before beginning her career in television. Alongside her longtime partner Billy Costa, she serves as co-host of NESN's *Dining Playbook*, *Meet Boston with Billy and Jenny*, and WBZ's weekly radio program "Food for Thought." Johnson is also the host of *Comcast Newsmakers* where she interviews policymakers and other prominent New Englanders. Deeply involved in the community, Johnson serves on the board or advisory boards of Mass General Cancer Center, the Massachusetts Restaurant Association, and Camp Harborview. Johnson recently went back to school to become an Ayurvedic Practitioner and as mother of two young girls, is passionate about promoting the healing power of food.

BILLY COSTA

Photo by Mike Diskin

Billy Costa is a three-time Emmy Award-winning on-air talent and Hall of Fame radio broadcaster. Born and raised in Cambridge, Costa is an alumnus of the New Preparatory School in Cambridge and attended Merrimack College before transferring to Emerson College, where he graduated with a degree in English. Costa has served as the voice of Boston for over thirty years on KISS 108, currently co-hosting the popular *Billy and Lisa in the Morning Show* as well as the weekly KISS Top 30 Countdown. Alongside his longtime partner Jenny Johnson, Costa is the host of NESN's *Dining Playbook* and *Meet Boston with Billy and Jenny*. A father of three sons, Costa is involved with many charitable organizations, and serves as an emcee and auctioneer for many galas, fundraisers, and events.

BRIAN SAMUELS

Photo by Natale Fox Photography

Brian Samuels is a Boston-based food photographer with a passion for storytelling through his lens. Since 2010 he has captured stunning images for renowned restaurants, magazines, cookbooks, and national food brands, utilizing light and styling to present each dish in its most beautiful form. His work has been celebrated in the *New York Times*, *Bon Appetit*, and *Boston* magazine.

Thank you to the partnerships that made this book possible:

www.ingramcontent.com/pod-product-compliance
Lightning Source LLC
Chambersburg PA
CBHW042012060526
44119CB00113B/255